Ancient Weapons

HISTORY DETECTIVES

Ancient
Weapons

Explore the history of the first weapons of war

Will Fowler

southwater

This edition is published by Southwater

Southwater is an imprint of Anness Publishing Ltd
Hermes House, 88–89 Blackfriars Road, London SE1 8HA
tel. 020 7401 2077; fax 020 7633 9499; info@anness.com

© Anness Publishing Ltd 1999, 2002

Published in the USA by Southwater, Anness Publishing Inc.
27 West 20th Street, New York, NY 10011; fax 212 807 6813

This edition distributed in the UK by The Manning Partnership
251–253 London Road East, Batheaston, Bath BA1 7RL
tel. 01225 852 727; fax 01225 852 852
sales@manning-partnership.co.uk

This edition distributed in the USA by National Book Network
4720 Boston Way, Lanham, MD 20706
tel. 301 459 3366; fax 301 459 1705; www.nbnbooks.com

This edition distributed in Canada by General Publishing
895 Don Mills Road, 400–402 Park Centre, Toronto, Ontario M3C 1W3
tel. 416 445 3333; fax 416 445 5991; www.genpub.com

This edition distributed in Australia by Sandstone Publishing
Unit 1, 360 Norton Street, Leichhardt, New South Wales 2040
tel. 02 9560 7888; fax 02 9560 7488; sales@sandstonepublishing.com.au

This edition distributed in New Zealand by The Five Mile Press (NZ) Ltd
PO Box 33-1071 Takapuna, Unit 11/101-111 Diana Drive,
Glenfield, Auckland 10
tel. (09) 444 4144; fax (09) 444 4518; fivemilenz@clear.net.nz

A CIP catalogue record for this book is available from the British Library

Publisher: Joanna Lorenz
Managing Editor: Linda Fraser
Produced by Miles Kelly Publishing Limited,
The Bardfield Centre, Great Bardfield, Essex CM7 4SL
Publishing Director: Jim Miles
Editorial Director: Paula Borton
Art Director: Clare Sleven
Project Editor: Raje Airey
Editorial Assistant: Helen Parker
Design: Casebourne Rose Design Associates
Art Commissioning: Susanne Bull; Liz Dalby
Picture Research: Lesley Cartlidge; Libbe Mella

Previously published as *Exploring History: Ancient Weapons*

Picture Credits
The publishers would like to thank the following artists: Mark Beesley;
Vanessa Card; Rob Chapman (Linden Artists); Wayne Ford; Terry Gabbey;
Sally Holmes; Steve Lings (Linden Artists); Kevin Maddison; Terry Riley;
Eric Rowe (Linden Artists); Mike Sanders; Peter Sarson; Rob Sheffield;
Roger Stewart; Ken Stott; Mike White (Temple Rogers); John Woodcock.
Maps: Stuart Squires and Steve Sweet (SGA).

The publishers wish to thank the following for supplying photographs for
this book: Page 9 (T/L) Erich Lessing/AKG London; 16 (B/L) E.T. Archive;
24 (T/R) AKG London; 32 (B/R) British Museum/E.T. Archive;
34 (T/R) E.T. Archive; 47 (B/L) Mary Evans Picture Library;
53 (T/R) E.T. Archive; 57 (T/R) Mary Evans Picture Library;
57 (B/L) Mary Evans Picture Library; 59 (B/L) E.T. Archive; 61 (T/R) Mary
Evans Picture Library. All other photographs from Dover Publications and
Miles Kelly archives.

1 3 5 7 9 10 8 6 4 2

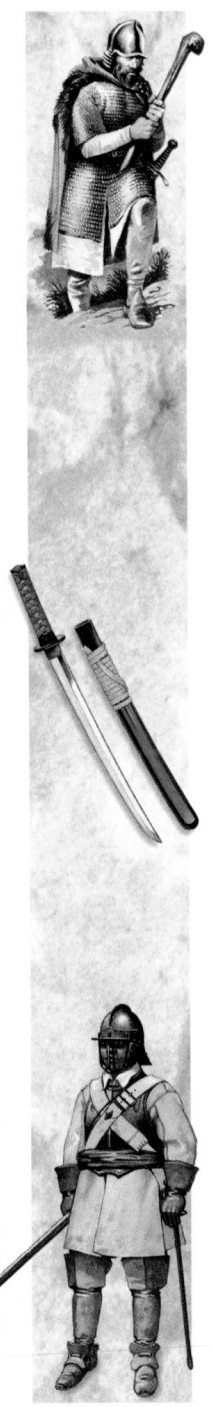

CONTENTS

Introduction

THE USE OF WEAPONS is almost as ancient as humanity. Many early weapons came from hunting tools such as spears and bows, but probably the oldest and most useful weapon is the knife or dagger. A flint dagger from Scandinavia and dated around 1800 B.C. is one of the earliest examples found in Europe, but daggers have been made from stone, bone, wood, metal and plastic. Today, soldiers are armed with bayonets or combat knives, weapons whose origins can be traced back to the simple dagger.

The development of weaponry and warfare runs alongside the development of early civilizations. As Stone Age people moved out of caves and simple shelters they banded together to form tribes and clans and built villages. Bronze replaced stone and flint for tools, and then iron replaced bronze. People began to acquire valuable possessions such as food stocks and animals, agricultural equipment, clothing and cooking utensils, and finally precious and attractive adornments and decorations. For the first time, weapons were needed, not just for hunting, but for self-defense and attack against other humans. The horses which herdsmen used to move cattle also allowed armed warriors to travel further and faster than people on foot. Raids and ambushes by horsemen, as well as movements by nomadic mounted tribes, became part of daily life.

To reduce the chance of death or injury, men used shields and armor, made from toughened animal hide,

▲ ARMOR
This Japanese warrior wears armor made from bamboo wood. Today armor is made from plastic or nylon.

▼ KEY DATES
The panel charts the progress of weapons and warfare from the Stone Age to the 1600s.

▼ FORTIFICATION:
Legionaries patrol Hadrian's Wall. Once territory had been wor or taken, rulers neede to defend their lands o empires. Castles and walls guarded by troops were built all over Europe.

THE FIRST WEAPONS

10,000–5000 B.C. Cave paintings in Spain show men armed with bows in combat.

3500 B.C. The Royal Standard of Ur, Sumerian pictures made from shells and precious stones, shows men armed with clubs, axes and spears.

2500 B.C. First fortified city, Ur of the Chaldees in Modern Iraq.

1680 B.C. The Hyksos introduce horse-drawn chariots to Egypt.

Assyrian siege towers

1800 B.C. Flint daggers made in Sweden.

Hittite chariot

1600 B.C. Bronze weapons in Sweden and Greece.

1469 B.C. The first record of a battle, at Megiddo, between Egypt and the Canaanites.

1000 B.C. Assyrians make use of iron for weapons.

500 B.C. In China, Sun Tzu writes the first book on military theory.

GREEKS AND ROMANS

Mediterranean galley

490 B.C. The Battle of Marathon fought between the Greeks and the Persians. Both army and navy are used and the Greeks defeat an enemy once thought to be unbeatable.

401 B.C. Battle of Cunaxa between Greeks and Persians uses chariots with scythes near Babylon. The Persians won.

387 B.C. First siege of Rome by Gauls. The City is burnt but the government buildings remain.

327 B.C. Alexander the Great crosses the river Hydaspes and defeats the Indian king Porus.

216 B.C. Hannibal of Carthage uses elephants at the Battle of Cannae against the Romans. It was his greatest victory.

206 B.C.–AD220 Crossbows widely used in China.

A.D. 408–410 The Goths under Alaric besiege Rome and sack it on August 24, 410.

Roman legionary

ANIMALS
Before the invention of the combustion engine, animals—usually horses—were used to transport troops, weapons and supplies. In the Crusades in the Middle Ages, both European knights and Saracen warriors fought on horseback. A medieval knight wore such heavy armor that he had to be lifted onto his horse by crane.

wood or wood strengthened with metal. This ancient equipment forms a model for the plastic shields used by modern-day police to protect themselves from the oldest of weapons—the thrown stone. The breastplates worn by ancient cavalries are copied by the "flak jackets" worn by many soldiers and helicopter crews today.

Tribal raids to steal goods or settle territorial disputes led to the building of fortifications. The fences and ditches built to control wild or domesticated animals were just as effective against raiding parties. Wood was easy to get and to work with, but could be set on fire by attackers, and would rot in time. Stone or mud brick was tougher and more enduring. Today, fortifications may no longer be towering castles, but we still use sandbag parapets, trenches and bunkers.

Ancient weapons relied for their effectiveness on human or animal strength although heavy shields and armor made maneuvering awkward. Warfare stayed much the same until the late 1800s when the internal combustion engine was invented.

TECHNOLOGY
Gunpowder was probably invented in China in the 10th century. The Arabs made the first known guns in about 1300. From the 1400s, muskets were developed in Europe and were gradually improved to allow them to be carried into battle.

VIKINGS TO THE MIDDLE AGES

500 Saxon raids on Britain from north Germany.

778 Battle of Roncesvalles. The Franks under Charlemagne beaten by Basques and Gascons.

700s to 1000s Norse raids on Britain and Europe.

The Norman conquest

1066 The Battle of Hastings. William of Normandy invades Britain and seizes power.

1095–99 The First Crusade. European Christian armies fight for the Holy Land.

1120 Welsh archers use longbows for the first time at Powys.

1190 Mongols under Genghis Khan begin expansion south and west from the Gobi Desert.

1330 First steel produced by accident in the Middle East while making iron.

1326 First illustration of cannon appears in manuscripts in Europe.

1337 Hundred Years War between England and France begins.

Medieval cannon

GUNPOWDER AND AFTER

1400 Handguns first produced in Europe. *Hand cannon*

1400–1600 Rise of halberdiers and pikemen in Europe. Simple breech loading guns in use.

1411 Earliest illustration of a simple matchlock.

1415 Battle of Agincourt. The last great victory of the longbow.

1420s Jan Zizka and the Hussites pioneer the use of war wagons and shoulder-fired guns.

1453 Massed artillery used by Turks at the Siege of Constantinople.

1500 Metal shot gains widespread use.

1505 First battleworthy pistol developed in Germany.

1547 Flintlocks developed in Spain.

1595 English begin to use fire arms and cannon.

1635 Flintlocks perfected in France.

1620 Swedes first use light leather-bound cannon. First tactical use of artillery.

Clubs, Maces, Hammers and Flails

THE EARLIEST KIND of weapons were clubs, maces and hammers. People could hold them in their hands. They could not break down and nothing could go wrong with them. The club is the oldest weapon. The earliest clubs were lumps of stone picked up from the ground. Prehistoric people used them as both tools and weapons. Clubs could be used to crush seeds for food. They could also be used as weapons to hunt animals or to fight with enemies. In South Africa, there are wall paintings made around 6000 B.C. showing two human figures with long heavy sticks that look like clubs. People made clubs from a variety of materials—long, heavy animal bones, or thick lengths of wood taken from trees, bushes or plants, for example.

When people learned how to make bronze, iron and steel, they used these metals to make stronger weapons. Using metal, the simple club was turned into a mace. A mace had a weighted, spiked

▲ CLUBS AND MACES AT HASTINGS
The Bayeux tapestry showing Norman cavalry, armed with maces and clubs, at the Battle of Hastings in 1066.

or pointed end. This could be used to batter through an enemy's shield or armor. It could be used in hand-to-hand fighting or by soldiers on horseback. Today in the United States, a ceremonial mace, made of ebony and silver, is used in the House of Representatives. In Britain, the scepter carried by the queen on special occasions is also a kind of mace.

The war hammer was like an ordinary carpenter's claw hammer, but had only one claw. This was a kind of spiked pick. The shaft, or handle, of a war hammer was up to a yard in length. A soldier using a hammer could reach out from his saddle to strike his enemy. Using the sharp claw of the hammer, the soldier could then puncture his enemy's metal helmet. This kind of blow to the head could be fatal, killing instantly.

The flail was first used by farmers to thresh corn. It was made into a weapon which is a mixture of mace and club. Between one and three lengths of chain were attached to one end of a thick metal stick. Weighted spikes were attached to the end of each length of chain. When the flail was used, the chains whipped through the air, and struck the enemy in several places at once.

▲ THE MACE
This elaborately crafted mace is a weapon of war but may also serve as a symbol of political or military status.

SIMPLE WEAPONS FOR CLOSE COMBAT
In its most primitive form, a club or contact weapon extends the reach of a person in close combat and replaces their feet or fists as weapons. It can be made from any spare wood or timber. Later the use of metal and the positioning of the weight at one end made these contact weapons much more effective in battle.

◀ THE SHILLELAGH
This Irish chieftain holds a shillelagh, a type of club made from hard wood like blackthorn or oak. Clubs are the simplest of contact weapons. In a more sophisticated version, they are still used today in the form of police night sticks.

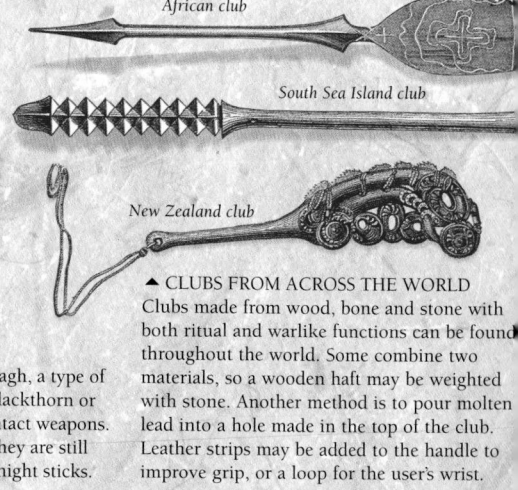

African club

South Sea Island club

New Zealand club

▲ CLUBS FROM ACROSS THE WORLD
Clubs made from wood, bone and stone with both ritual and warlike functions can be found throughout the world. Some combine two materials, so a wooden haft may be weighted with stone. Another method is to pour molten lead into a hole made in the top of the club. Leather strips may be added to the handle to improve grip, or a loop for the user's wrist.

◄ THE ROUT OF SAN ROMANO
This detail from a painting by the Italian Renaissance artist Uccello shows armor-clad horsemen wielding maces, hammers and bows.

▲ HAMMER VERSUS MACE
Even though medieval knights wore complicated armor, they still fought with simple weapons. In this picture you can see how the hammer and mace were used, and how powerful they look.

16th-century war hammer

▲ WAR HAMMER
The spike on the war hammer was designed to penetrate armor. The flat end was used for smashing in helmets.

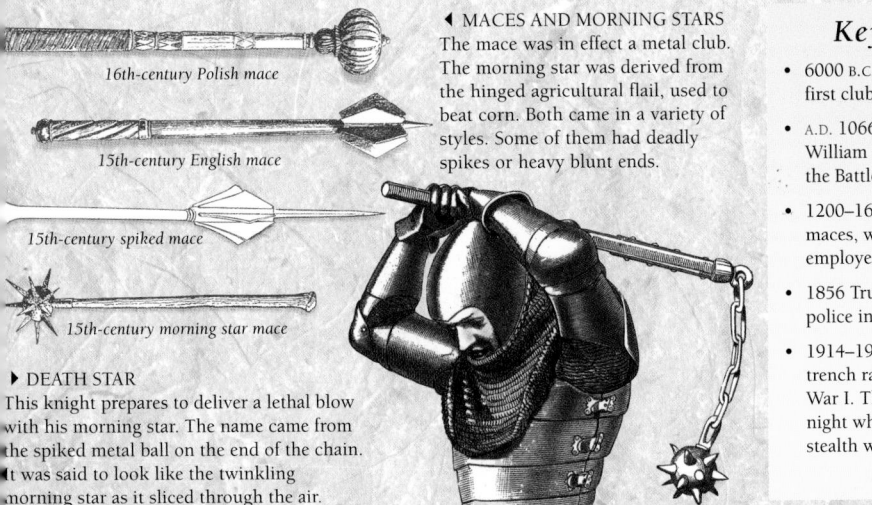

16th-century Polish mace

15th-century English mace

15th-century spiked mace

15th-century morning star mace

◄ MACES AND MORNING STARS
The mace was in effect a metal club. The morning star was derived from the hinged agricultural flail, used to beat corn. Both came in a variety of styles. Some of them had deadly spikes or heavy blunt ends.

▶ DEATH STAR
This knight prepares to deliver a lethal blow with his morning star. The name came from the spiked metal ball on the end of the chain. It was said to look like the twinkling morning star as it sliced through the air.

Key Dates

- 6000 B.C. Cave paintings of first clubs in Africa.
- A.D. 1066 Bishop Odo and William I carry maces at the Battle of Hastings.
- 1200–1600 Morning stars, maces, war hammers employed in battle.
- 1856 Truncheons used by police in Great Britain.
- 1914–1918 Clubs used in trench raids during World War I. They were used at night when silence and stealth were vital.

Axes and Throwing Weapons

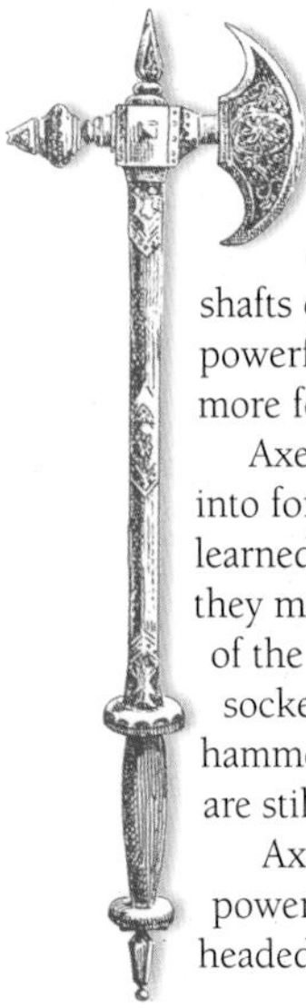

THE AX WAS FIRST USED as a woodsman's tool for felling trees. The first axes, like the first clubs, were made from sharp stones or flints. They were simply cutting tools. Later they were fixed to shafts or handles, which made them more powerful. They could be swung first to put more force behind the blow.

Axes were first made by tying sharp flints into forked or split branches. When people learned how to use bronze, iron and steel, they made stronger, sharper axes. By the time of the Iron Age, ax heads could be cast with a socket to fit the handle. Then the blade was hammered and ground to a sharp edge. Axes are still made in the same way today.

Axes have always been symbols used by powerful kings and rulers. The double-headed bronze ax was used as the symbol of the Minoan civilization in Crete. Pictures of the ax were used in wall paintings and as decoration on pottery.

The hand ax had a short handle. It could be used to hack the enemy in hand-to-hand combat. Soldiers could also throw the ax, although

▲ DECORATIVE AX HEADS
The simple wedge shape of an ax head has often been decorated for war or ritual throughout the world.

◀ KNIGHT WITH AX
Medieval knights often rode into battle armed with a heavy battle-ax. This had a sharp blade and a spike. The ax was attached to the knight's arm with a chain. These axes could cause terrible injuries to both men and horses.

this meant they might lose it. A good example of a fighting ax was the tomahawk used by Native North Americans. Tomahawks were first made of stone, then later of steel brought by traders. They were used for hunting and fighting. The tomahawk had a long handle which gave it a powerful swing. British soldiers fighting in North America in the 18th century adopted the tomahawk for their own use.

The last time an ax was used in combat in Europe was at the battle of Waterloo in 1815 between the

THROWING WEAPONS
The simplest hand-thrown weapon is the sharp-edged stone. However, metal and wood are more effective. The Franks of the 5th and 6th century used an iron throwing ax called a Francisca. Native North Americans used the tomahawk up to the 19th century.

Australian boomerangs

◀ CHAKRAM
The Sikhs of India used a razor-sharp steel war-quoit or chakram, which they used to throw at the enemy. Chakrams were in use as late as the 19th century.

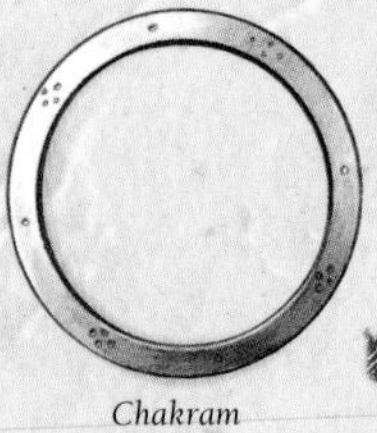

Chakram

◀ BOOMERANGS
War boomerangs do not return to the thrower, unlike the hunting version. Their sharp edges wound or stun the opposition.

NORSE RAIDERS
Norse raiders disembark from their longships and race into action armed with their single-headed war axes. These iron-bladed weapons were often elaborately decorated.

French and the British, together with the Prussians. During the battle, French troops used axes to break down the door of the farm at Hougoument, which was being held by the British infantry.

The ax is still in use today. In some armies, it is the badge of the assault pioneers. These are soldiers who do engineering work. The badge shows crossed axes. Firefighters also use axes which look rather like ancient war axes. They have spikes and blades and are easy to hold and use in one hand.

THROWING KNIFE
The leaf-shaped throwing knife was a war weapon used throughout Africa from Nigeria through the Congo to the Sudan. As it turned through the air in flight the blades of the throwing knife were intended to strike the victim in a sawing action. The disadvantage of a throwing weapon was that if it missed, it could be thrown back.

African throwing knife

◄ WAR BLADE
This African throwing knife had a steel, double-edged blade. The short handle was bound with grass or a leather thong to give the warrior a good grip. The knife was designed purely as a weapon, unlike an everyday knife, and could not be used off the battlefield for day-to-day tasks or hunting.

Key Dates

- 2000–1700 B.C. Double-headed ax used as symbol for the civilization of Minoan Crete.

- 700 B.C. Evidence that slings were used in Assyria.

- A.D. 400–500 Francisca throwing axes found in England.

- 700–1100 Single- and double-bladed axes used by Norse raiders.

- 900–1400 Heavy, long-handled battle-axes used by knights.

- 1700s Iron-bladed tomahawks manufactured for North America.

- 1800s Chakrams in use in India.

Slings, Bows and Crossbows

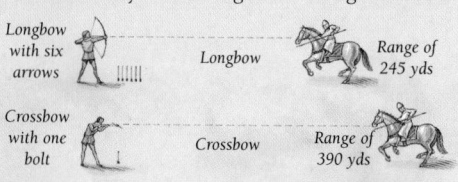

▲ DAVID AND THE GIANT GOLIATH
The shepherd David defeated the Philistine warrior Goliath by stunning him with a sling stone.

THE SLING, LIKE the longbow and crossbow, is a "stand-off" weapon. This lets a soldier attack his enemy while remaining out of reach himself. Slings were used in early sea battles. Piles of sling stones were discovered at Maiden Castle, Dorset, England, where the Celtic defenders fought the Romans in A.D. 44.

Bows are among the most ancient weapons in the world. Ancient cave paintings, dating from 10,000 and 5000 B.C., from Castellon in Spain show figures of men using bows for fighting. Bows have been found in Denmark dating from 2000 to 1500 B.C. and in Egypt from around 1400 B.C.

The bow was also used for hunting. Many of the skills of the hunter were also those of the warrior. Experienced archers could fire accurately from horseback or chariot.

In the 16th century, Henry VIII of England ordered that young men should practice shooting their bows every Sunday after church. Most bows were made from yew wood.

The triumph of the English and Welsh longbow was in three battles against France: Crécy in August, 1346;

Poitiers in September, 1356; and Agincourt in October 1415. English and Welsh archers were able to keep the French mounted nobles under a constant rain of arrow from 800 feet. As horses and riders crashed to the ground, others became entangled with them and they all became easy targets.

When muskets and rifles were first invented, the longbow, fired by a skilled archer, was still more accurate. It was not until the American Civil War that firearms became more effective. Muskets were adopted because it was easier to train soldiers to use them.

◀ TAKING AIM
A crossbowman takes aim. He operated the trigger, which held back the string with a hook called a nut, with his right hand. If the weapon was used to hunt game a stone was used in place of the bolt.

◀ TAKING COVER
A crossbowma takes cover wi his weapon an equipment stowed in a shield carrier.

STAND OFF WEAPONS

The crossbow and longbow allowed ordinary foot soldiers to engage enemies at long range. This meant that mounted knights and foot soldiers could be killed before they could use their swords, lances or axes. Both longbows and crossbows could penetrate armor at short range, which meant that they could bring down a knight in full armor.

Using the Crossbow

Longbow with six arrows

Longbow

Range of 245 yds

Crossbow with one bolt

Crossbow

Range of 390 yds

Spanning

Fitting the bolt

Taking aim

▲ SHOOTING RANGE
The expert longbowman could fire up to six aimed arrows in a minute to a range of about 245 yards, or twelve less accurately.

On the other hand, the skilled crossbowman had a longer range at 390 yards, but a far slower rate of fire. He could only shoot one bolt a minute.

▲ THREE STAGES
It took much longer to load a crossbow than to aim and fire an arrow. There were three stages to loading and firing a crossbow. Spanning was the first stage. It involved pulling

the bow string back and locking it. Then the bolt was fitted into the slot. Finally the bow was aimed and fired. With mechanical assistance as many as four bolts could be fired in a minute.

▼ LONGBOWS IN ACTION
English and Welsh longbowmen
protected by a palisade of stakes fire
at advancing French knights.

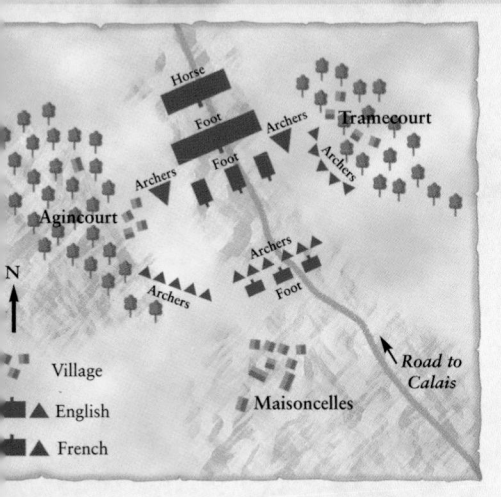

Some armies used men armed with crossbows. The crossbow is a short bow attached to a piece of wood or metal called a stock. The bowstring was pulled back by hand or mechanically and held in place by a hook and trigger mechanism. The short arrow, or bolt, was fitted into a slot and aligned with the string. The crossbowman had only to aim and operate the trigger.

The first description of a crossbow appears in a book called The Art of War by the Chinese military thinker Sun Tzu, writing in 500 B.C. In 1139 Pope Innocent II tried to ban the use of the crossbow against Christians because of the terrible injuries it caused. Richard I of England died in 1199 from gangrene caused by a crossbow bolt.

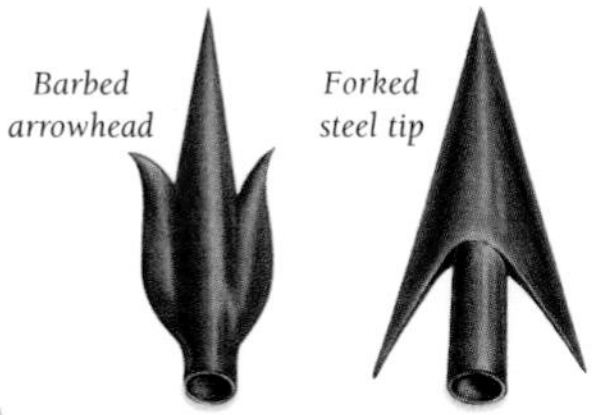

Barbed
arrowhead

Forked
steel tip

▲ ARROWHEADS
Archers used different shaped arrowheads. Barbs and forks were popular. Barbs ensured that the arrow stayed lodged in the target and made withdrawal difficult. The forked steel tip was used in the Far East.

Horse
Foot
Archers Tramecourt
Archers Foot
Archers
Agincourt
Archers
Archers
Archers Foot
Road to
Calais
N
Village
Maisoncelles
▲ English
▲ French

◀ LONGBOWS
SAVE THE DAY
The Battle of Agincourt was the last great victory of the longbow against mounted soldiers. Wet weather slowed down the French knights and the English and Welsh archers stopped two attacks before Henry V's forces attacked from the rear. The French were defeated and lost about 5000 of their men.

Key Dates

- 10,000–5000 B.C. Cave paintings in Spain show archers in battle.

- 500 B.C. Sun Tzu writing about military doctrine mentions crossbows.

- A.D.1100 Crossbows widely used in Europe.

- 1199 King Richard I of England killed by a crossbow at Chaluz.

- 1200s Longbow enters wide use in England and Wales.

- 1914–1918 Crossbows used for firing grenades in the trench warfare during World War I.

Daggers and Knives

SMALL, LIGHT AND EASY TO CARRY, daggers and knives are hand-held weapons. Daggers and knives make very good secret weapons as they can be used in complete silence. They were used on their own for hand-to-hand fighting, or for throwing.

Although the dagger design was based on the knife, there is an important difference between the two. The knife is a simple tool, sharp along one edge of the blade, it may have

a relatively blunt point. It can be used for everyday tasks like cutting up meat for example, as well as being used as a weapon. A dagger is double-edged and tapers along its length to a sharp point. It may have a guard between the blade and the handle to protect the user's hand. It is always classified as a weapon.

The earliest daggers were made from flint. Early daggers were also made from sharpened wood or bone. Daggers made from bronze, iron and steel lasted longer.

◀ SWORD AND DAGGER
A fully armored knight equipped with a sword and dagger. The sword was suitable for hacking and the dagger for thrusts to gaps in the armor.

▶ MURDER WEAPON
Lurking in the shadows, an assassin armed with a stiletto awaits his victim. This dagger was easy to conceal and deadly if it penetrated a vital organ.

Stiletto

DAGGER DESIGN

As a weapon, a dagger or knife was inexpensive and very effective in even unskilled hands. It could be used for agricultural or domestic work if necessary. A dagger consists of the blade, the cross guard that protects the user's hand and knuckles, the grip or handle and the pommel. In a fight, the pommel at the base of the grip could be used in the same way as a hammer on an opponent's head. Dagger designs vary from country to country. The Indian katar or push dagger was designed to be used in a punching action.

Pommel

Grip or handle

Blade

◀ A BLADE FROM THE BRONZE AGE
This Swedish dagger dates from around 1350–1200 B.C. and shows all the basic design principles of a hand-held edged weapon. It has a separate riveted hilt, distinct pommel and double-edged blade with fullers or blood grooves. Later designs would have a full-length tang, an extension of the blade, built into the handle. This gave the dagger greater strength and better balance.

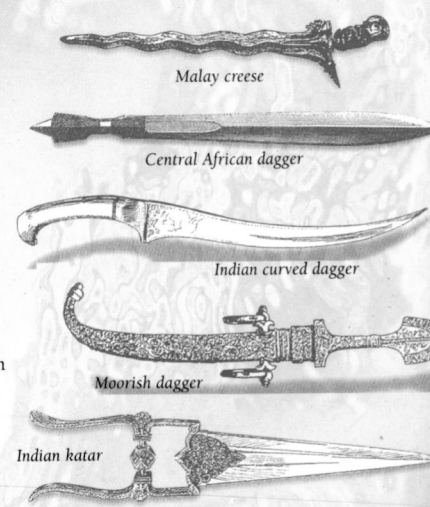

Malay creese

Central African dagger

Indian curved dagger

Moorish dagger

Indian katar

► A DUEL
Duels were considered an honorable way to settle an argument. The stilleto is used here to block the sword thrust.

In the 14th and 15th centuries sword fighters used daggers with their swords. A swordsman would hold the dagger in his left hand to block and deflect his enemy's sword. He would then make a thrust with the sword in his right hand.

Swordsmiths were the people who made swords and daggers. The daggers they made were almost works of art. They had beautiful inlays and precious and semi-precious metals and jewels set in the handles. The best known swordsmiths were the Saracens of Damascus in Syria. They used a method of hammering layers of steel together. This made blades of swords and daggers very hard and sharp and created a pattern rather like watered silk, known as Damascene.

In the 20th century the dagger and the knife are still used by soldiers in combat. In World War I the United States Army was issued with the Fighting Knife Mk 1 which protected the user's knuckles with a guard which could be used as "knuckle dusters" or "brass knuckles." Modern combat knives are more like multi-purpose tools, with a screwdriver, saw edge, and wire cutter as well as a sharp knife blade.

▲ TOLEDO, CITY OF STEEL
This Spanish city was a center for beautifully designed swords, daggers and armor which were manufactured for many centuries and exported through Europe.

► SWORDBREAKER
A 17th-century Italian swordbreaker was a dagger made for special use in a sword fight. It was designed to trap an opponent's sword thrust in its notched blade. The dagger would not be used just to parry a sword thrust. A vigorous twist of the wrist could either break the thin blade of the trapped sword, or wrench it from the user's hands.

Cross guard

Notched blade

Key Dates

- 2000 B.C. Bronze daggers were manufactured throughout Europe.

- 500 B.C. First Iron Age weapons produced and used widely.

- A.D. 1600s–1700s Stiletto manufactured in Italy. It was copied and used throughout Europe.

- 1700s–1900s Dress daggers worn as part of military or political uniforms.

- 1820s Bowie knife invented in the United States by Jim Bowie. Its classic design forms the model for most modern sheath knives.

- 1940s–1990s Combat knives issued to soldiers as multi-function tools.

Swords, Sabers and Scimitars

ONE OF THE MOST ANCIENT weapons in the world, the sword is now a symbol of rank for officers on ceremonial parades. Tools shaped like swords were used in farming work and to cut down trees. Like other working tools they were adapted to use in fighting. The kukri from Nepal is an ancient weapon that remains in service today with Gurkha regiments of the British army. Its broad, curved blade is ideal for chopping and even digging, but it is also a very good weapon for close combat.

Early swords were used to slice rather than to thrust. For many centuries European swords had a short, straight blade which tapered to a point. It was sharp on both edges. They were first made in bronze, later iron and finally steel. The short Roman steel

sword called a gladius was about 20 inches long. It was like a long, wide-bladed dagger. The gladiators who fought in the Roman circus or arena with these swords, got their name from the gladius.

Swords in the Middle Ages were longer. They were about 30 to 35 inches long with a cross-shaped handle and tapering blade. Long swords could be used to thrust at the enemy but most soldiers fought by hacking at each other. Swords could be used by soldiers on foot or horseback.

Very strong men used the two-handed sword, which was very long, with a broad blade. Swordsmen used both hands to fight with it. Scottish chieftains in the mid-16th century used a long, double-edged, two-handed sword called the claidheamh múr, or claymore.

▲ VIKING WEAPON
A Viking sword from the 10th century. Its hilt is covered with silver leaf.

◀ TWO-HANDED
Medieval knights in close combat. One of them is armed with a hand-and-a-half, or two-handed sword.

▲ SWORD SKILLS
A Japanese samurai warrior from the 15th century. Samurai warriors usually wore two swords and a distinctive headdress.

SWORDS
Swords today are made from steel and have been made from bronze, stone and even wood. Although not used in war, in many cultures, they remain the symbol of power and status within military organisations. Sword fighting techniques vary according to the design of the blade. The Japanese favor a chopping action, while the thin bladed rapier is best suited to a thrust.

▶ SAMURAI WEAPON
The Japanese traditionally used single-edged daggers and swords of different lengths. The traditional long-bladed sword is called a katana.

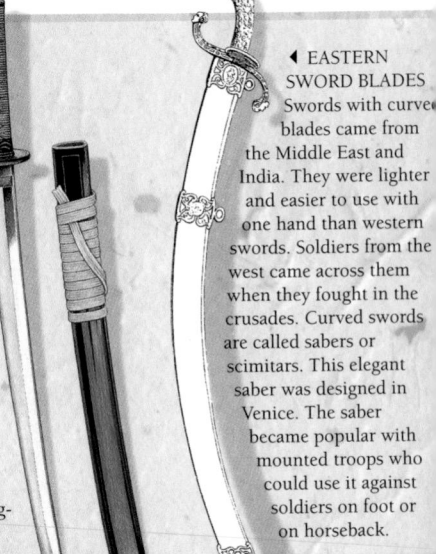

◀ EASTERN SWORD BLADES
Swords with curved blades came from the Middle East and India. They were lighter and easier to use with one hand than western swords. Soldiers from the west came across them when they fought in the crusades. Curved swords are called sabers or scimitars. This elegant saber was designed in Venice. The saber became popular with mounted troops who could use it against soldiers on foot or on horseback.

◀ DEATH AT DAWN
A Victorian print shows the victor of a duel armed with a rapier. His victim's weapon shows the guard or side rings designed to protect the hand.

▶ HEAVY BLADE
An Asian warrior armed with a bow and broad-bladed sword. The sword has the weight closer to the tip, which makes it ideal for a chopping action.

Knights and soldiers discovered the sword-making techniques of the Middle East during the crusades. This ...d to improved sword design in the west. Soldiers in ...e Middle East used a curved sword called a scimitar. ...hese had long, narrow blades and very sharp edges.

The guard in front of the sword handle was made to ...rotect the fighter's hand. Around 1600, Venetian sword ...akers produced a new guard design called the basket ...ilt. This was a curved, perforated guard that protected ...e whole hand. The basic design is still used today on ...any modern ceremonial swords.

The mounted soldiers of the cavalry charged towards their enemy with their swords pointing forward for a straight thrust. However, long swords became difficult to use once the soldiers were fighting close to each other. There was no room to make a good stroke. The saber was developed as a cavalry weapon. It had a short, curved blade and was used to slash and thrust. The blade cut as it went up and as it came down.

In Renaissance Europe, noblemen and courtiers wore weapons almost as fashion accessories. Rapiers were very popular. These were light, very narrow swords known with elaborate guards. The fashion lasted from about 1530 through to 1780.

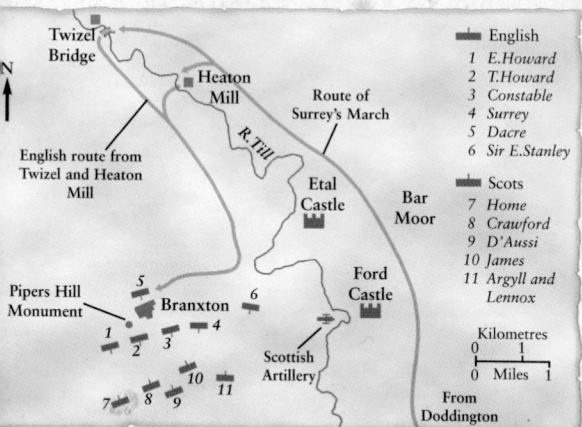

English
1 E.Howard
2 T.Howard
3 Constable
4 Surrey
5 Dacre
6 Sir E.Stanley

Scots
7 Home
8 Crawford
9 D'Aussi
10 James
11 Argyll and Lennox

Kilometres
0   1

0   Miles   1

From Doddington

THE BATTLE OF FLODDEN 1513
...his battle between the English and the Scots, took place in Northern ...gland. The Scots fought with the two-handed claymore sword.

Key Dates

- 1300 B.C. Bronze swords used in war.

- 650–500 B.C. Iron swords in use.

- A.D. 900s Viking double-edged swords used in Viking raids all over Europe.

- 1300s Curved Turkish sabers in use as a cavalry weapon.

- 1500s Rapiers in use.

- 1500s Scottish two-edged swords in use.

- 1600s Venetian basket-hilt swords in use throughout Europe.

- 1850 Kukri in use with Nepalese soldiers.

Spears, Poles, Pikes and Halberds

PREHISTORIC HUNTERS used spears to kill animals for food. They were more powerful and accurate than simple stones and could be thrown from safe distances. The earliest spears were simply straight saplings (very young trees) which were sharpened at one end. In the Far East, bamboo wood was used. It was light and strong and could be hardened in a fire to give a very sharp point. Flint, stone or metal points fixed onto a spear made it even more effective.

There were soldiers armed with spears in most ancient armies. Another name for the throwing spear is javelin. Throwing spears have one drawback. Once they have been thrown at the enemy, you cannot get them back. In fact, the enemy may use them to throw at you. The Romans solved this problem by inventing a spear called a pilum. This had a long, thin neck near the point. When the spear hit a target, it snapped at the neck. Then it could not be used by the enemy.

Longer, heavier stick weapons were used to fight with rather than to throw. In medieval times, country people used large sticks called staffs for walking. Various types of blades were attached to these to make weapons for both cavalry and

▲ THE QUARTERSTAFF
This was the simplest weapon ever made. It could be cut from saplings. In Europe in the Middle Ages, the staff was used more in competitions and brawls than in war.

▶ PIKE WALL
Pikemen in the 17th century lined up to form a barrier for cavalry. This tactic gave musketeers time and space to reload their weapons behind the pike wall.

POLE ARMS

The advantage of pole arms like spears, pikes or halberds is that the user can stab, chop or even entangle his enemy at a safe distance. Peasants often fitted a pruning bill to the shaft of a quarterstaff to make a simple pole arm during revolts and insurrections.

◀ PIKEMAN
A pikeman in the splendid uniform of the 17th century. In addition to his helmet, he might also have a breastplate for extra protection. Some pikes were nearly 4.8m long, the same length as those used by the Macedonians around 350 B.C..

English halberd

Bill

Italian linstock

German glaive

English gisarme

nfantry troops. A spear point would make a lance, used by cavalry. Knife blades and axes were also used as well as billhooks, which were tools for cutting hedges. A trident was made by attaching a sharp-pointed fork (like a pitchfork). Halberds were long poles with a spear point and an ax head mounted behind it. Pikes were long, heavy pole weapons with long blades of various designs.

In the 14th and 15th centuries, the Swiss developed specialized pike tactics. Using a pike that consisted of a twenty-foot shaft and a three-foot iron shank, Swiss soldiers marched in columns which had a front line of 30 men but could be 50 to 100 men deep. The massed pikes could stop a cavalry attack. Many rulers and generals hired Swiss pikemen to fight in their battles. Today, the Pope's Swiss Guard, armed with pikes, is all that is left of this force.

The bayonet fitted to the muzzle of modern army rifles is based on the pike. Bayonets were first used by soldiers with muskets. Although muskets were effective firearms, they took time to reload. By attaching long pointed blades, called bayonets, to their muskets and forming themselves into a hollow square with bayonets pointing outward, soldiers could break up a cavalry attack and protect each other while they reloaded.

◀ SWISS GUARD
The Swiss Guard at the Vatican still carry pikes and wear uniforms similar to those worn in the 15th and 16th centuries.

▶ CLOSE COMBAT
Two soldiers fighting with halberds. One tries to use the curved beak to trip his enemy while the other uses the spike as a spear.

▶ ON THE MOVE
An Etruscan warrior armed with a sword and throwing spear. The classic tactic for these lightly-armed men was to throw their spears, then to run forward as the spears were in flight. By the time the spears reached their target, the Etruscan soldier was within sword reach. The enemy was hit twice in one move.

▲ ISLAND WEAPONS
Spears have been used throughout history in many different cultures. This islander from New Caledonia in the Pacific Ocean is ready to throw one spear and holds two more in reserve.

Key Dates

- 600 B.C. GREEK hoplites use short throwing spears.

- 350 B.C. The sarissa (light spear) used in Macedonian phalanx formations.

- 200–100 B.C. Roman foot soldiers use the pilum, or heavy javelin.

- A.D. 900–1400 Lances used by knights for jousting and war in Europe.

- 1400s Pole ax enters service.

- 1400–1599 Halberd widely used.

- 1600s Pikes enter service.

- 1815 Cavalry lances adopted by Britain from France.

Ancient Firearms

IREARMS ARE WEAPONS that use gunpowder and shot. The earliest firearms in the west were made around the beginning of the 15th century. They worked like mini cannons and were small enough to be carried by a soldier on foot or on horseback. They looked a lot like the modern hand-held flare used to signal an emergency at sea. They had a short barrel attached to a handle.

▲ MATCHLOCK
The matchlock was used in Europe until the 18th century and in parts of India until as late as the 20th century.

▶ MOUNTED FIREPOWER
The wheellock was ideal for mounted soldiers who would need to keep one hand free.

By the late 15th and early 16th centuries, the standard firearm was about five feet long with a barrel, stock and butt. The stock supported the metal barrel and the butt rested in the crook of the firer's shoulder when the gun was being used.

The arquebus was a bigger weapon, often used mounted on a simple tripod. It usually needed two people to operate it. One aimed it and the second put a lit taper into the touch hole or vent. The soldiers who had to carry these heavy weapons were very eager for craftsmen to make them lighter and easier firearms. The matchlock was the first improvement. This weapon was fired using a fuse or length of cord which had been soaked in a chemical called saltpeter. This made it burn slowly. The cord was coiled into a curved lever called a serpent. A shallow pan filled with gunpowder had a thin tube leading into the barrel of the weapon. To operate the matchlock, the soldier lit the cord, opened the spring-loaded cover to the

HAND GUNS
Improved metal technology and designs made hand guns more reliable and easier to carry. Tactics for infantry and cavalry changed to suit these firearms. Weapons were still made by craftsmen. After the Napoleonic wars, muskets and guns began to be mass produced.

▲ POWDER HORN
Gunpowder was stored in a powder horn to keep it dry. Many of them were made from hollow animal horns. They had a spout through which an exact measure of powder was dispensed.

▶ HAND MADE
The lead ball fired by muskets was easily made using a simple mold. Once the molten lead had hardened, the handles of the mold were opened and the new ammunition was ready. Soldiers made their own ammunition as needed.

Mould

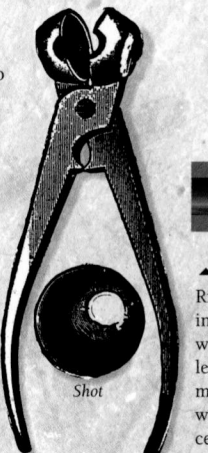

Shot

Inside a rifled gun barrel

Bullet spinning fr the barre

▲ RIFLING
Rifling was a system of grooves inside the barrel of a firearm which gave the bullet a spin as it left the barrel. This made the gun more accurate. Rifled weapons were still rare in the early 19th century. Now rifling is used in every modern gun.

◄ **MUSKETEERS**
Musketeers armed with the heavy Spanish style matchlock weapon that required a fork rest for easy handling. This weapon was used by armies throughout Europe from about 1567 for over 100 years and the musketeers were an elite within the army.

► **WHEELLOCK**
This firearm used a spring-loaded wheel and pieces of iron pyrites to produce sparks which ignited the gunpowder at the moment of firing. But they were expensive and not in common use.

pan and then pulled the trigger. This brought the burning cord, or match, down into gunpowder, which exploded.

The matchlock was not a practical weapon for a soldier on horseback who needed to have one hand on the reins. So the wheellock was developed. It worked like an old-fashioned cigarette lighter. When the trigger was pulled the pan of gunpowder was uncovered. A metal wheel rubbed against a lump of iron

pyrites and produced a stream of sparks. A mounted soldier could carry two or three short-barrelled wheellock pistols in holsters on his saddle or tucked into the tops of his riding boots.

The snaphaunce, miguelet and flintlock were later firearms. They used flint and steel to produce a spark. The flintlock was in use until the mid-19th century. A shot could be fired every 20 seconds from a smoothbore flintlock musket, but the weapon was inaccurate beyond 85 yards.

◄ **AX MAN**
An ingenious combination of wheellock pistol and hatchet probably produced in the 16th century. Handguns of this period were often beautifully decorated with inlay and engraving.

Ax head

Ax head

▲ **PISTOL BAYONET**
A flintlock pistol made between 1788–90 which gave the firer the back up support of a short, bayonet-style blade.

Grill

Blade

Gun barrel

▲ **SHIELD GUN**
This shield has a matchlock pistol in it. It was probably made around 1544–47. The grill above the barrel allows the user to take aim while safely under cover.

Key Dates

- A.D. 1411 Earliest illustration of simple matchlock.
- 1518 Wheellock banned within Holy Roman Empire.
- 1540 First pistols made.
- 1550 First examples of rifling developed .
- 1570 Spanish musket in widespread use.
- 1610 Flintlock developed.
- 1650 Flintlocks in widespread use.
- 1700 Matchlock no longer widely used in Europe.

Armor

SOLDIERS WORE ARMOR to protect the head, neck, eyes and chest. Early armor was made from bronze. Later iron and steel were used. Japanese warriors wore armor made from bamboo wood. There is a problem with armor. It must be thick or heavy enough to protect the soldier wearing it, but light enough for him to move around easily.

The ancient Greeks were the first to use bronze armor. They used it to protect their forearms, legs and chest. A Roman legionary wore armor which covered his chest, stomach, back and shoulders. This protected his lungs, heart and the important blood vessels in the neck. Although his arms and legs were not protected, he could still move and run quickly and easily.

A cheap way to make armor was to sew metal plates onto a heavily padded tunic. By the time of the Battle of Hastings in 1066, nobles and soldiers wore chain or link mail. It protected them from sword, arrow or spear thrusts. It could also

move with their bodies. Mail was made by linking iron rings together to make a kind of metal fabric. Norman and Saxon soldiers both wore a tunic that covered the arms and body as far as the knees. A hood made from mail covered the head. Underneath ring mail, soldiers wore padded jackets. This stopped the mail being pushed into their skin by the force of a sword thrust.

Plate armor became very popular in medieval Europe. The whole body was covered with plates that were either strapped on to the wearer or hinged off one another. This was called a suit of armor. Each suit was made to fit exactly. Although the metal was heavy, its weight was so well balanced that a knight could walk about in reasonable comfort when wearing it. The parts of the armor that were most likely to be struck by a sword were specially angled so that

▲ ANCIENT ARMOR
A figure dressed in classical armor of Greece and Rome with a breastplate covering his torso and shinpads called greaves protecting his lower legs.

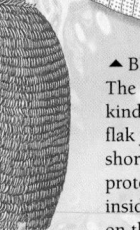

▲ JAPANESE WARRIOR
Japanese armor consisted of bamboo plates sewn to a padded jacket. Mythical motifs decorated the helmet.

PROTECTION
Chain mail was both light and sword-proof, but was never as strong as plate armor. The answer to this problem, for many centuries, was to use chain mail in areas such as the neck and limb joints and plate armor in slabs on the chest, back, legs and arms. The top of the head was protected by plate armor.

◀ NORMAN MAIL COAT
A Norman soldier wearing chain mail coat and helmet, light and flexible armor made from linked steel rings.

◀ INDIAN MAIL HELMET
This helmet uses a combination of plate and chain or ring mail to protect the head and neck. It is similar to the helmets worn by the Saracens.

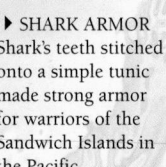

▶ SHARK ARMOR
Shark's teeth stitched onto a simple tunic made strong armor for warriors of the Sandwich Islands in the Pacific.

▲ BRIGANDINE
The brigandine was a kind of 16th century flak jacket. It was a short, flexible coat with protective rivets on the inside and a rich fabric on the outside.

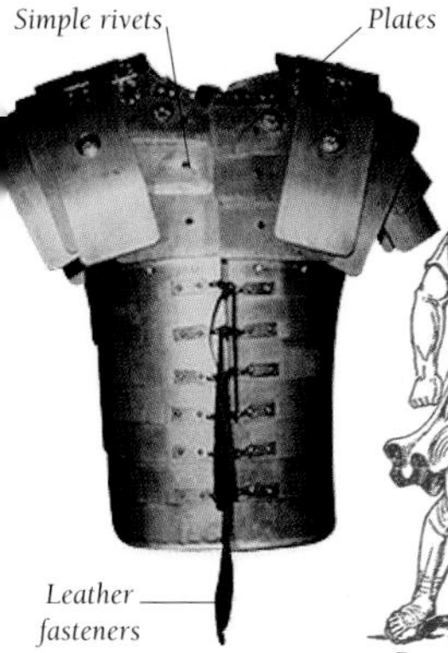

Simple rivets   Plates

Leather
fasteners

he sword blade would slide off without
oing harm.

This kind of armor was very expensive. Both the
*n*ight who owned it and the armorer who made it
*w*anted it to look beautiful as well as to work well.
*I*t was engraved and inlaid with metals such as
*b*rass and even gold. Enamel was used to
*c*olor the metal plates so that knights
*a*ppeared in black, green or even red armor.

Even though plate armor was worn in medieval
*t*imes, soldiers still used chain mail to protect parts of
*t*he body that armor could not cover. Later, cavalry
*t*roopers, armed with sabers and ready to engage in
*h*and-to-hand fighting, wore chain mail around their
*n*ecks to prevent their throats being slashed open.

◀ ROMAN BREASTPLATE
Roman armor was made of plates
held together with bronze hinges. In
later versions, these were replaced by
simple rivets and strong hooks.

Roman foot soldier

◀ MOUNTED ARMOR
Knights might be well
protected, but their horses
could easily get hurt in
battle. To protect them,
they wore their own
armor.

The same care and
attention that went into
making armor for the
knight was given to that for
his horse. How much armor
they both wore and how
richly it was decorated,
showed the owner's wealth.

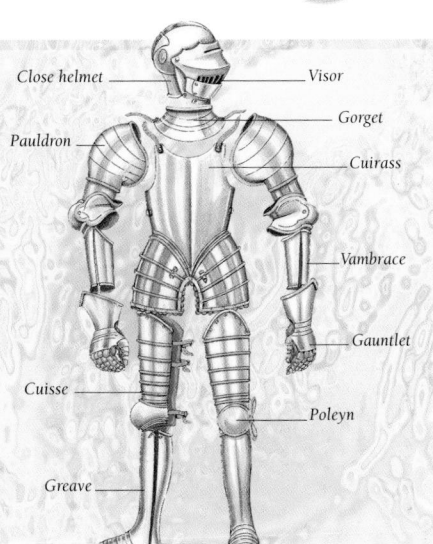

▶ A SUIT OF ARMOR
*K*nights had their armor
*es*pecially made to fit. Armor
*w*as made up from lots of
*s*eparate pieces. It was laced
*o*r strapped together and
*h*ung off a gorget. This was a
*m*etal collar that protected the
*n*eck and shoulders. A suit of
*a*rmor from the 16th century
*w*as made up of at least 16
*p*ieces and took a long time to
*p*ut on. Knights needed a
*s*quire to help them get ready
*f*or battle. Armor was very
*h*eavy but, it was so cleverly
*m*ade that the knights could
*s*till move around fairly easily.
*M*ost of the names of the
*p*ieces of armor are from the
*F*rench language.

Close helmet ———   Visor

Pauldron ———

Gorget

Cuirass

Vambrace

Gauntlet

Cuisse ———

Poleyn

Greave ———

Key Dates

- 1500–1200 B.C. Bronze Mycenaean armor.

- 460 B.C. Corinthian armor.

- 102 B.C. Mail armor used by Romans.

- A.D. 75–100 Roman legionary interlocked plate armor widely used.

- 1100s Norman mail armor.

- 1300s Jointed plate armor.

- 1500s Horse armor widely used.

- 1600s Pikemen' s armor.

- 1990s Body armor made from plastic or nylon is used today by police forces and armies.

Shields

▲ GREEK PROTECTION
A Greek hoplite of 600 B.C. equipped with a round bronze hoplon shield. Bronze was easy to work, but was softer than iron.

BODY ARMOR was part of the wearer's "clothing". A shield was a piece of moveable armor. It was normally carried by or strapped to the left arm, while a weapon was held in the right hand. It could be used to push aside an opponent's sword or spear. Like all armor, a shield has to be strong enough to defend its user yet light enough for him to carry easily. It also has to be made in a shape that will give the user most protection.

The earliest shields were made from animal skin stretched over a wooden frame. They were something like the shields carried by African warriors in the 18th and 19th centuries.

The first metal shields were made of bronze. The ancient Greeks used large round shields. In ancient Britain, Celtic warriors used round bronze shields and figure-of-eight shaped shields. Circular shields were used by cavalry in both ancient Greece and Rome. Round

▲ RIOT PROTECTION
Modern German police with polycarbonate riot shields and helmets as protection against rocks in riots.

▼ GALLIC SHIELD
The Norman inverted tear-drop shaped shield covered the torso, but left the legs free.

shields were used later by the cavalry in the armies of the Middle and Far East. The Vikings also had round shields.

Roman legionaries used an oblong shield that was slightly curved. It was large enough to protect a man from his shoulders to his knees. The shields could fit together. A group of legionaries lined up in rows of four could fit their shields together and form a very strong barrier. Used in this way, the shields made a kind of temporary tank.

SHIELDS
Shields could be used to block a sword blow or protect the head and shoulders from arrows. The Greeks and Romans had finely crafted shields. In medieval times, shields were plainer but made from tougher materials.

◀ INSIGNIA
Knights wore insignia on their shields and armor to identify themselves on the battlefield. Here a simple bar and two dots are repeated, like a brand name, on the knight's shield, lance and the trappings of his horse.

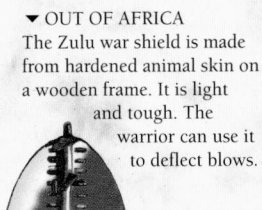

▼ OUT OF AFRICA
The Zulu war shield is made from hardened animal skin on a wooden frame. It is light and tough. The warrior can use it to deflect blows.

▶ CELTIC CRAFT
The bronze Celtic shield is like a Roman design. The metal decoration on the front shows the wealth and position of the shield's owner.

▲ THE TOUGH TORTOISE
The Roman interlocked shield pattern called a tortoise allowed troops to approach the enemy fortifications under cover. Soldiers would then climb on their shields to attack the enemy walls.

Well protected, the whole unit moved forward to attack with their short swords.

The Romans developed a shield technique for attacking walls and castles. The soldiers fitted their shields together above their heads making what was called a testudo, or tortoise. Once the "tortoise" had reached the walls of the castle, the shields provided a platform for men to climb up to the fortifications.

By the time of the Norman invasion of Britain in 1066, shields had changed to a distinctive kite shape. The shield tapered downward, so the user could move his legs, but protected his upper body. Both cavalry and infantry used this type of shield.

The medieval shields were smaller. English and Welsh archers used a small round shield while knights had shields which were flat along the top edge and tapered to a point. This shape is now the accepted pattern for modern heraldry. It was in this period that shields were painted with the coats-of-arms of their users so they could be recognized by their followers on the battlefield.

▲ MOON POWER
The raised symbols of the sun and moon on this Persian shield were meant to give extra power to the user.

▶ ANCIENT PERSIAN SHIELD
This shield from Persia has cut-outs at arm level. These allowed the soldier to attack with his spear while he was still protected by his shield.

◀ BUCKLER SHIELD
This round German shield called a buckler has decorative studs called bosses set in an unusual random pattern.

Key Dates

- 1750-1600 B.C. Wood and hide shields used by Mycenaean soldiers.

- 480 B.C. Bronze and wood shields used by Athenian hoplites.

- 400 B.C. Celtic shield fittings found in England.

- 400 B.C. Hide shields replace bronze types for Athenian troops.

- 300 B.C. Roman soldiers equipped with hide and wicker shields.

- A.D. 1000–1200 Norman and Norse troops use tear-drop shields.

- 1400s Shields with coats-of-arms used by knights.

Helmets and War Hats

▲ SAXON HELMET
This helmet from the 7th century comes from the Saxon burial ground at Sutton Hoo. It is inlaid with silvered bronze.

Soldiers have always worn helmets of some kind to protect their heads and eyes in combat. They came in all shapes and sizes, to suit the kind of weapons soldiers were likely to come up against. Ancient helmets were designed to protect soldiers from attack by cutting weapons such as swords or thrusting weapons such as spears or arrows. Some helmets were simple round metal hats. Others were more like iron masks. The ancient Greeks invented the nosepiece. This was a strip of armor running from the brim of the helmet along the bridge of the nose. It was still in use in the 17th century. The Romans favored helmets with deep cheek pieces. These were hinged flaps that hung down the sides of the helmet, covering the ears and cheeks, but leaving the front unrestricted. This made it easier for the wearer to see clearly as he was fighting.

In the 11th century, the Normans wore conical helmets with nosepieces. They also wore a chain mail hood which completely covered the ears and back of the neck. This gave them added protection.

PROTECTING THE HEAD

Because the head incorporates the brain and face with important organs such as the eyes, ears, nose and mouth, it has always been protected in war. Helmets were made from bronze, iron or steel. Today they are made from modern plastics and polymers, which are light but very strong.

◀ THE GREAT HELM
By the mid-14th century the helm was the helmet most widely used by mounted knights. A visor pulled down to protect the face. Helms often sported elaborate crests at the top showing the owner's coat-of-arms. Today's motorcycle helmets resemble the helm.

Assyrian war hat

Hoplite helmet

Assyrian helmet

▲ ANCIENT HELMETS
Helmets began as simple metal hats. Later, hinged flaps were added to give protection to the cheeks, nose and neck without making it too difficult for the soldier to see or move. The flaps were often decorated.

◀ SPEED OR STRENGTH
During the crusades of the 11th and 12th centuries, European knights, who wore heavy armor and helmets, met Saracen warriors who wore lighter mail coats and small helmets that fitted close to their heads.

The most magnificent helmets were made during the medieval period in Europe. Ordinary foot soldiers had simple armor including a plain helmet but royalty and noblemen had splendid armor and helmets. The helmets were engraved and inlaid and were made with angles to deflect sword blows and a hinged visor that protected the wearer's eyes. A three-dimensional model of the family crest was often set on top. These elaborate helmets were like badges to show the nobility of the wearer.

By the time of the English Civil War (1642–1651), helmet design had changed. There was neck and earflap protection, a hinged peak and a face guard. The helmet was known as a "lobster-tail pot" because it looked like a lobster shell.

When the helmet was revived in World War I, the British army adopted the style of the brimmed war hat worn by archers at the Battle of Agincourt (1415). It was called the "kettle."

▶ LOBSTER POT
The pot or lobster-tail pot helmet worn by Parliamentarian cavalry in the English Civil War gave them their nickname of "Roundheads."

▶ MEDIEVAL HELMETS
Armorers in the Middle Ages produced helmets and armor for wealthy and discriminating customers. Some designs were very fanciful. Others had carefully constructed angles and shapes which could deflect sword or mace blows.

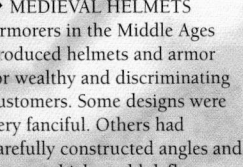

English 13th century

French 15th century

French 12th century

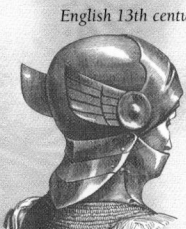
French 13th century

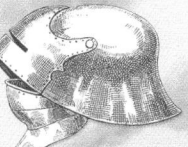
German 15th century

Key Dates

- 1700–1100 B.C. Bronze helmets in use in Mycenae.
- 55 B.C.–A.D. 100 Roman cavalry and infantry helmets introduced.
- 1000–1100 Norman helmets with nosepiece.
- 1300s Basinet hinged helmet.
- 1350s Helms in use by European knights in battle and in tournaments.
- 1400s Kettle-hat or war hat.
- 1500s Nuremberg close helmets.
- 1600s Pot or lobster-tail pot helmet worn by Cromwell's Roundhead army in the English Civil War.

Animals at War

ELEPHANTS, HORSES, DONKEYS, bullocks and camels have all been used to fight wars. Most of them were used to carry soldiers or pull wagons. Elephants were used rather like modern tanks. An elephant could trample enemy soldiers, while archers riding in a large basket on its back could pick off targets with their arrows.

▼ HANNIBAL'S TANKS
The most famous elephants in war belonged to Hannibal the Carthaginian general. In 216 B.C. h brought them from Spain to fight against Rome a the battle of Cannae in southern Italy.

WAR BEASTS
Elephants are not aggressive by nature but could be used to frighten troops who had never seen them before. A panicking elephant could trample its own soldiers. In India, handlers called mahouts carried a spike. If their elephant went out of control, they killed it.

◀ ELEPHANT POWER
The elephant has three natural weapons: its great weight, its huge tusks and its powerful trunk.

▲ THE HEAVY BRIGADE
Elephants were used on the front line of battle to frighten the enemy infantry and to block cavalry charges. Like modern tanks, they were protected from close range attack by special groups of foot soldiers.

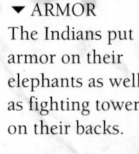

▼ ARMOR
The Indians put armor on their elephants as well as fighting towers on their backs.

One of the earliest battles to use war elephants was fought at Arbela, now modern Irbil, in 331 B.C. The Persian leader Darius led an army, including 15 war elephants, against Alexander the Great of Macedonia. Alexander's troops were frightened of the elephants at first, but so well-disciplined that they did not run away but fought and won the battle.

War elephants had been used in India by the Hindus from around 400 B.C. They were as important as chariots on the battlefield. At the battle of Hydaspes in India in 327 B.C., Porus, the Rajah of Lahore, led elephants against Alexander the Great. This time, Alexander's horses were frightened by the elephants. However, his foot soldiers attacked the elephants with battleaxes. The animals panicked and the Macedonians won.

The most famous war elephants belonged to Hannibal, the Carthaginian general. He fought against Rome in the Second Punic War (218–203 B.C.). The elephants were used in several battles but Hannibal was eventually beaten.

Elephants were first seen in England in A.D. 43 when the Romans used them to invade. War elephants were still in use in India during the 18th century. The elephants had iron plates fixed to their heads and were driven forward like four-legged battering rams to break down the gates of the town of Arcot in 1751. They panicked when they were fired at.

▲ CAMEL ARMY
The camel has been used for transport in battle in the Middle East. It has lots of stamina and can move fast. Camels can also travel a long way without much food or water. Here, camel-mounted soldiers use lances and swords in a lively battle.

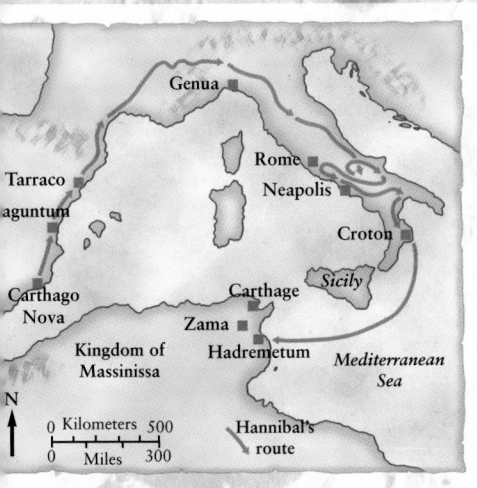

◀ OVER THE ALPS
Hannibal marched with his elephants across the Pyrenees and the Alps to attack Imperial Rome. When he set out from Saguntum in 218 B.C., he had 50,000 infantry, 9000 cavalry and about 80 elephants. By the time he reached the Po valley in northern Italy six months later, only a few elephants were still alive. Hannibal had lost 30,000 infantry and 3000 cavalry.

Key Dates

- 327 B.C. Battle of Hydaspes. Alexander the Great meets Indian elephants.

- 275 B.C. Battle of Beneventum, Italy. Carthage uses elephants for the first time against Rome.

- 218 B.C. Hannibal crosses the Alps.

- 202 B.C. Battle of Zama. Hannibal defeated and his elephants taken.

- 190 B.C. Battle of Magnesia. Syrian war elephants panic and confuse their own troops.

- A.D. 43 Roman Emperor Claudius uses elephants to invade Britain.

Horses in Battle

ORSES MADE IT POSSIBLE for armies to move around quickly. They could pull wagons and siege weapons or carry loot and possessions. On the battlefield, they could be ridden by scouts or messengers taking news to and from the generals planning the battle. Large horses, working together as heavy cavalry, were unstoppable on the battlefield.

The first people to use the horse in war were the Assyrians around 800 B.C. They used them as cavalry, to pull chariots and for hunting. The Romans bred from European, Middle Eastern and African stock to produce racehorses, hunters, chargers and harness-horses.

The saddle with stirrups, which were probably invented in China, reached Europe in the 2nd century AD and transformed mounted operations forever. They made it easier to ride a horse. A Roman soldier on foot could cover about 5 miles a day. When he was on a horse, he could travel twice as far as that.

The horse also made it possible for groups of peop to move far away from their home lands. In the 13th century, the Mongols roamed from Central Asia as far as Vietnam, the Middle East and Europe.

There were two kinds of cavalry, the light and the heavy. The difference between them was based on the size of the horse. Most ancient armies had both light and heavy cavalry. About two-thirds of the Mongol riders

▲ PARTING SHOT
Horse archers from Parthia, a ancient country now part of Iran, used to pretend to retrea then turned and fired their arrows backward to take the enemy by surprise.

◀ A LIGHT SKIRMISH
Persian light cavalry troops, carrying round shields and armed with lances and maces, fight a running battle.

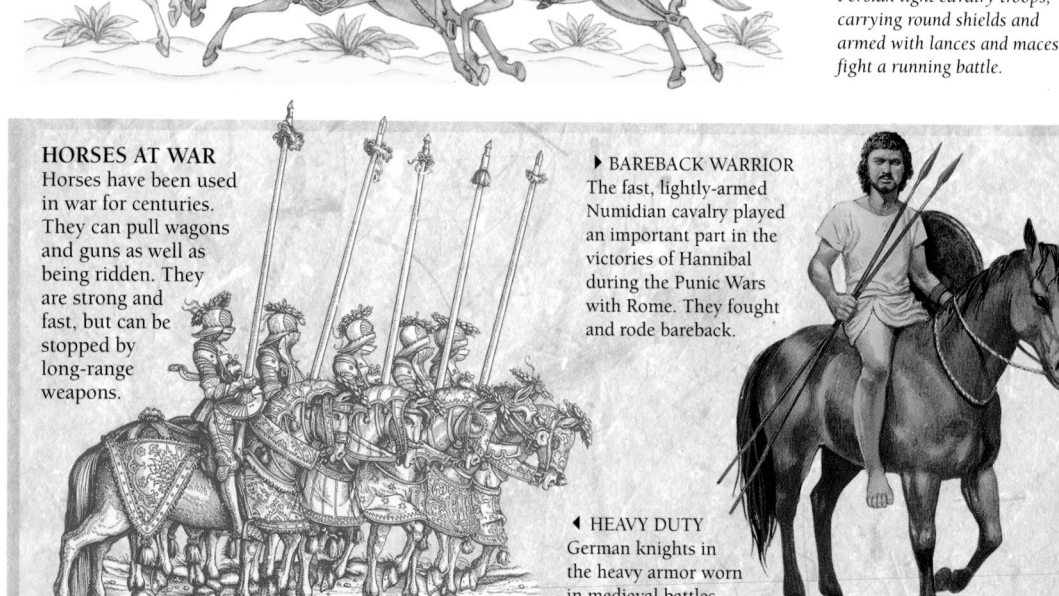

HORSES AT WAR
Horses have been used in war for centuries. They can pull wagons and guns as well as being ridden. They are strong and fast, but can be stopped by long-range weapons.

▶ BAREBACK WARRIOR
The fast, lightly-armed Numidian cavalry played an important part in the victories of Hannibal during the Punic Wars with Rome. They fought and rode bareback.

◀ HEAVY DUTY
German knights in the heavy armor worn in medieval battles. This protected both horse and rider.

▼ JOUSTING TOURNAMENT
*Today, tournaments and battles are
re-enacted by "knights" on horseback.*

▶ AT THE
CHARGE
*The horse wears
a piece of head
armor called a
chauffron. Its
spike is almost
as much of a
weapon as the
rider's lance. Both are
pointed toward the enemy
when the horse charges.*

were light cavalry. They had small, fast horses, wore
protective helmets and carried bows and arrows. The
heavy cavalry had big, strong horses, wore mail armor
or heavy leather clothing and were armed with lances.

Armies in medieval Europe had only foot soldiers
and knights on horseback. To carry a knight in full
armor the horse had to be big and strong. The knights
were a kind of heavy cavalry. By the 16th century the
armies of Europe had concentrated on heavy cavalry.
The French called them gendarmerie and the Germans
called them Schwarzreiter or "Black Riders." It was
when they fought with Turkish armies in the 17th
century that Europeans began to see how useful a light
cavalry could be and to set up light brigades of their

own. The Hungarian light cavalry, called hussars, wore
Turkish-style uniforms.

The heavy cavalry wore helmets and breastplates,
rode large horses and carried a pistol and heavy saber.
The light cavalry had no armor and rode horses chosen
for their speed. The riders carried two or even three
pistols and a light sword.

The Tulughma

Heavy Cavalry — Light Cavalry

◀ MONGOLIAN
WAR TACTICS
The Mongolian
army used light and
heavy cavalry and
many different
tactics. This one is
the tulughma. The
heavy brigade led
the charge and
broke up enemy
lines. At the same
time they protected
the ranks of light
cavalry behind
them. When the
enemy ranks were
broken, the lighter
horses ran through
or around their
own heavy ranks.

Key Dates

- 500 B.C. Persians employ lancers and horse archers.

- 53 B.C. Parthian horse archers defeat Romans at Carrhae (modern Iraq).

- A.D. 100s Stirrups are introduced.

- 200–400 Horse archers and lancers used by Romans.

- 977–1030 Mahmud of Ghazni uses cavalry horse archers in north India.

- 1000–1200 Crusaders use Moslem mercenaries called Turcopoles.

- 1396–1457 French cavalry, gendarmes, in action.

- 1500–1600 German "Black Riders" in action in Europe.

Chariots and War Wagons

horses, the archer riding beside him was free to concentrate on fast and accurate firing at the enemy. Not all chariots were two-man vehicles. If there was only one rider, he would tie the reins around his waist to keep his hands free so he could use his weapons. Some chariots, pulled by three or four horses, could carry several men, armed with a variety of weapons. Used all together, chariots could break up ranks of enemy infantry. Some later chariots had the protection of armor. They may also have had blades or scythes fitted to the hubs of their wheels to prevent enemy infantry or cavalry approaching too close. The drawback with chariots, like many wheeled vehicles, was that they could bog down in mud and it was hard for them to cross rough ground.

Between 1420 and 1434 the Hussites, a group of people from Bohemia

▶ EGYPTIAN TACTICS
An Egyptian courtier on a hunting trip fires his bow and arrows from a moving chariot. The same skills would be used in war.

CHARIOTS WERE A CLEVER WAY to combine speed and action. Most of them were pulled by horses. The driver was called a charioteer. For the armies of ancient Egypt, Assyria, Persia, India and China, chariots were the weapon of surprise, racing in and out of battle. Most chariots held two people, the driver and the bowman. With the driver to handle the horse or

▲ ROMAN CHARIOT
The chariot was not used a great deal in war. It was a popular sight at the public Games held in Rome and other major cities of the Empire.

▲ WARRIOR QUEEN
Boudicca, chieftain of the British tribe called the Iceni, used war chariots in her battles against invading Romans.

WHEELS OF WAR

Chariots were first used in the Bronze Age in the 15th century B.C. in the Middle East. They could be pulled by two to four horses, but the larger number were harder to control. They could move easily on the flat deserts of Egypt and around the Euphrates, but they were not ideal transport in muddy, broken or rocky terrain. The war wagons used by the Hussites in Europe in the 15th century A.D. were almost like the first tanks. They were formed into circles like mobile forts. Soldiers fired cannons and muskets from the shelter of the wagons.

▲ LEONARDO'S TANKS
Leonardo da Vinci, the genius of the Renaissance, had many ideas that were ahead of his time. This sketch shows armored vehicles of various kinds. They look like early versions of modern tanks.

▼ GUN CARRIAGES
In 15th-century Europe, horses and carts were used to haul heavy cannons around the battlefield. This meant that the guns could be taken to positions where they could be most use. As artillery troops became more mobile, they could do more harm to the enemy.

German cavalry at bay. There were 350 wagons in a Wagenburg, linked together with chains and sometimes dug in. Within the circle of wagons were 700 cavalrymen and 7000 infantry. Gaps closed with chains, posts and spikes could be opened to allow the Hussite cavalry out to attack. When the Hussites brought in cannon mounted on special wagons, the German cavalry refused to attack them any more because they were too dangerous.

Some historians have suggested that the Hussite Wagenburg was the first tank in history as it combined fire power, protection and movement.

now the Czech Republic), fought with the Germans. he Hussites were followers of the religious reformer ohn Huss. Their army, commanded by Jan Zizka, used rmored carts. The wagons were formed into a circle of agons called a Wagenburg, or wagon castle. Behind he wagons, crossbow archers and musketeers kept the

Key Dates

- 1400 B.C. Chariots used by Egyptians.

- 331 B.C. Persian chariots armed with scythes at Battle of Arbela.

- 327 B.C. Indian chariots used at Battle of Hydaspes.

- 225 B.C. Last use of chariots by Celts in Battle of Telamon, Italy.

- A.D. 60 Boudicca uses chariots against the Romans in Britain.

- 378 Romans use wagons to defeat Goths at Adrianople (modern Turkey).

- 378 Fighting wagons used by Jan Zizka and the Hussites.

▶ CHARIOTS OF MARBLE
any artists have made paintings and sculptures of chariots. This Roman ulpture of a chariot and a pair of frisky horses is in the Vatican Museum.

Cavalry Weapons

THE WEAPON USED BY A MOUNTED soldier reflected his skills as a rider. The Mongol cavalry riders of Genghis Khan could ride without reins, which meant they were able to use a bow while in the saddle. The lance or spear could be used in one hand. It was long enough for a rider to reach enemy foot soldiers. Cavalry normally rode straight at their enemy using the speed and impetus of the horse to add weight to the lance thrust. The cavalry lance became popular in medieval Europe and continued to be used in battle by horsemen in Poland and Hungary. Polish Lancers used it against the French during the Napoleonic Wars in 1800–1815. Medieval knights used the lance in battle, and practiced their skill in tournaments. The knight's horse also became a target, so craftsmen began to make armor for horses.

Horse armor was called bard. At its simplest it was made up of the chauffron, a plate covering the front of the horse's skull, and the peytral which covered the breast above the front legs. Full horse armor included the crupper and the flanchard. The crupper covered the horse's rump. The flanchard was an oblong plate fixed to the base of the saddle. It protected the horse's flanks and closed the gap between the crupper and peytral.

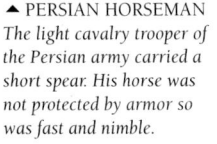

▲ PERSIAN HORSEMAN
The light cavalry trooper of the Persian army carried a short spear. His horse was not protected by armor so was fast and nimble.

▲ SAMURAI BOWMAN
Japanese samurai warriors did not only use swords. Many were also masters of the longbow. A mounted archer on a trained horse had two advantages. He could move fast and he could fire his weapon from a distance, out of the range of his enemy's swords and lances.

THE HORSE AT WAR
The horse changed combat forever. On horseback, soldiers could travel further and transport more equipment. They could also cover more ground on the battlefield. Stirrups gave the riders more control over their mounts, leaving their hands free for fighting in battle.

◀ MONGOLIAN PONY
Tough, fast little Asian ponies provided transportation and mare's milk for the Mongol warriors as they crossed Europe.

▲ HORSE ARMOR
Medieval horse armor protected the animal without slowing it down. The rider's legs covered its bare flanks in battle.

▲ A GREAT TEAM
Chain mail protects this horse's neck. The weight of horse, man and armor at the gallop swept them through the ranks of the enemy's foot soldiers.

▶ TOURNAMENT
When jousting for sport, knights used blunted lances so that they would not harm each other.

Chauffron

Blunted lance

Knight's insignia

European cavalry troopers had been using straight swords from Roman times. When fighting in the Middle East, European soldiers came across the curved sword, which was used as a pattern for the curved cavalry saber. This was ideal for the slashing backstroke.

The wheellock pistol was developed in the 16th century. It was designed to be used with one hand so that the rider could shoot while keeping full control of his horse. Because of the noise, flashing and smoke, horses had to be trained to carry men through gunfire.

▶ GOING WEST
In 1190 the Mongol emperor Genghis Khan led his great army westward. It was divided into groups of 10,000 men called hordes. The hordes were named after different colors. By the 13th century they had swept deep into eastern Europe and reached almost as far as Austria. They could not have gotten so far or gone so fast if they had not had such swift horses.

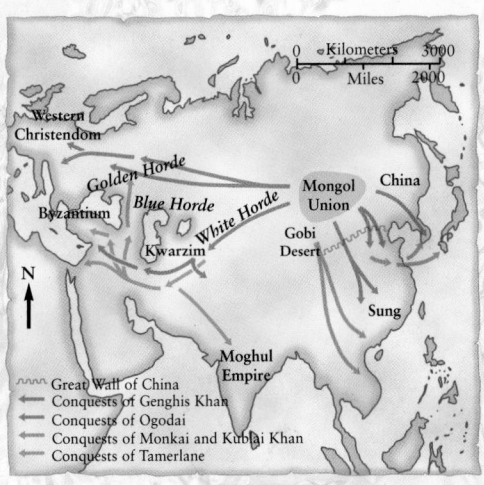

Western Christendom

Golden Horde

Byzantium

Blue Horde

White Horde

Kwarzim

Mongol Union

China

Gobi Desert

Sung

Moghul Empire

0   Kilometers   3000
0   Miles   2000

N

〰〰 Great Wall of China
← Conquests of Genghis Khan
← Conquests of Ogodai
← Conquests of Monkai and Kublai Khan
← Conquests of Tamerlane

Key Dates

- 400s B.C. Persian mounted archers.

- 400 B.C. Spartan cavalry armed with short javelins.

- 330s B.C. Alexander the Great uses mounted lancers.

- 200s B.C. Hannibal uses Numidian mounted lancers.

- A.D. 1200s Mongol hordes, mounted on horseback, invade Europe.

- 1300s–1500s Jousting lances in use.

- 1400s Heavy horse armor introduced.

- 1600s Sabers introduced as cavalry weapons.

Castles and Fortifications

THERE ARE NUMEROUS EXAMPLES of prehistoric and ancient fortifications throughout the world. The people who built them often used natural features such as hills, cliffs and crags or rivers, lakes and swamps to enhance their strength. Where these features were not present, people created them, making ditches, mounds and later walls and towers. Sometimes castle builders used earlier sites. For example, at Porchester in Hampshire, England, in the 1120s, Henry I built a motte-and-bailey castle using the square fortifications of an earlier Roman Saxon fort.

The outlines of square Roman forts can be seen throughout Europe. These forts were called castra, which is where we get the word castle. Castra were built

▶ THE MEDIEVAL CASTLE
This typical castle has crennelated walls, which meant the defenders could shoot through the gaps.

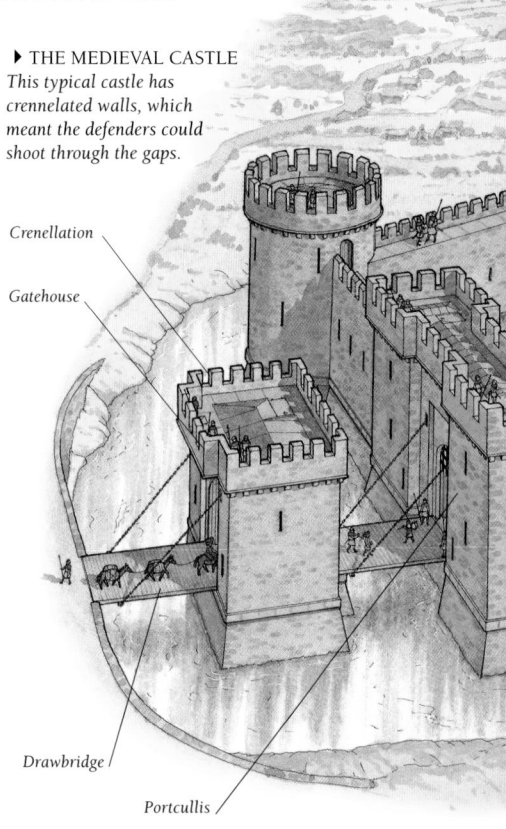

Crenellation

Gatehouse

Drawbridge

Portcullis

◀ SCOTTISH CASTLE
Caerlavarock Castle, Scotland, is a classic moated castle. The pattern of stone bricks on the top of the round towers is known as machicolation. It is to protect soldiers inside the towers as they fight off an attack. The moat which surrounds the walls gives even more protection. The castle was hard to storm.

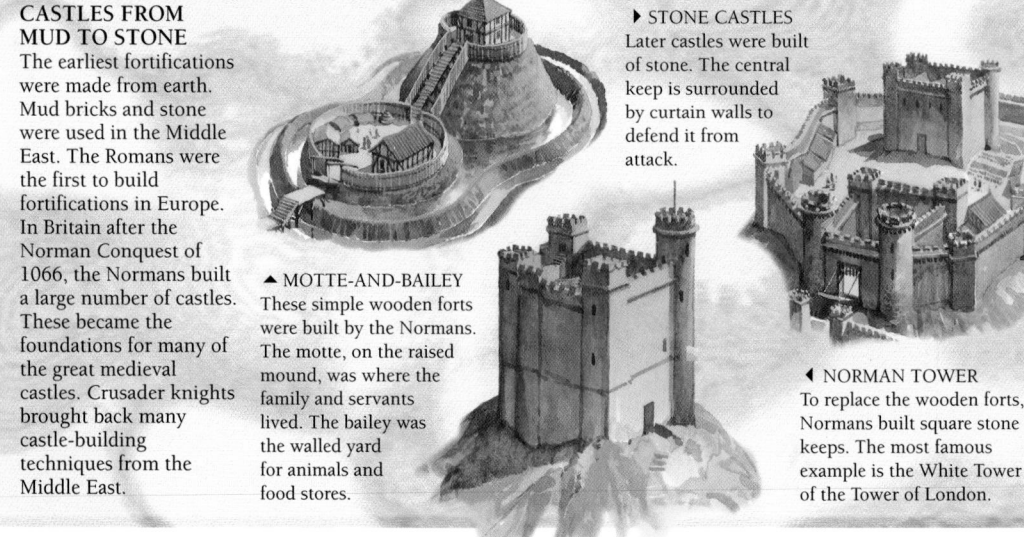

CASTLES FROM MUD TO STONE
The earliest fortifications were made from earth. Mud bricks and stone were used in the Middle East. The Romans were the first to build fortifications in Europe. In Britain after the Norman Conquest of 1066, the Normans built a large number of castles. These became the foundations for many of the great medieval castles. Crusader knights brought back many castle-building techniques from the Middle East.

▲ MOTTE-AND-BAILEY
These simple wooden forts were built by the Normans. The motte, on the raised mound, was where the family and servants lived. The bailey was the walled yard for animals and food stores.

▶ STONE CASTLES
Later castles were built of stone. The central keep is surrounded by curtain walls to defend it from attack.

◀ NORMAN TOWER
To replace the wooden forts, Normans built square stone keeps. The most famous example is the White Tower of the Tower of London.

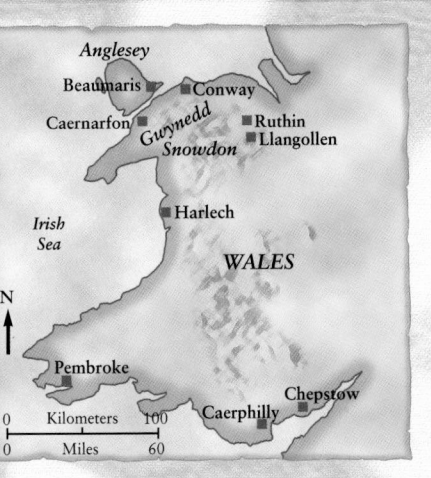

Keep

Curtain wall

Moat

by legionary soldiers as a secure base at the end of a march in hostile territory. Sometimes these temporary bases became more permanent. They were called Castra Stativa. Rations, stores and baggage could be dumped there while lightly-armed legionaries patrolled enemy territory.

Norman motte-and-bailey castles in England were built as bases for the occupying power after the defeat of King Harold at Hastings in 1066.

The medieval castle was a base for a lord or baron. It was defended by a large garrison of soldiers. Towns grew up around the castles and, if the community was wealthy, they would build strong walls around the outside. Knights and nobles who had fought in the crusades against the Saracens brought back many new ideas about castle design. The curtain wall surrounding the castle was a Saracen idea. For the baron in his castle or the citizens of a town, the time and resources expended improving the defenses were like an insurance policy against bad times.

◄ WELSH CASTLES
In the 13th century, King Edward I of England built a large number of castles in Wales. This was to strengthen his grip on the country. The Welsh people did not care for English rule. Craftsmen were brought from all over England to help in the building work. Edward's wife and queen, Eleanor, gave birth to their first son, the future Edward II, at Caernarfon Castle. He became the Prince of Wales, the first English man to hold the title.

Key Dates

- 2500 B.C. Ur of the Chaldees, first fortified city, built (in modern Iraq).
- 701 B.C. Jerusalem fortified.
- 560 B.C. Athens fortified.
- A.D. 1058–1689 Edinburgh Castle.
- 1066–1399 Tower of London.
- 1181–89 Dover Castle.
- 1196–98 Chateau-Gaillard built by Richard I in France.
- 1200s Krak des Chevaliers, a Crusader castle, built in Syria.
- 1538–1540s Henry VIII builds forts along England's south coast.

Towers, Keeps and Gates

TO DEFEND THEIR CASTLES people built tall towers and keeps. Standing at the top, they could see enemy ships or army columns a long way off. This gave the people in the castle time to prepare for attack. When the enemy arrived at the castle walls, the lookouts on the tower could see down into their camps or siege weapons and fire missiles at them.

Towers can be square or round, but always have very thick walls.

Towers are safe places to hide when an enemy attacks. In the 9th and 10th centuries, Vikings raided England and Ireland. To defend themselves, Irish people built high towers in villages or near monasteries. These stone-built towers had no outer defenses. They had arrow slits or embrasures and a simple door built high up the wall that could only be reached using a ladder.

After the Norman Conquest of England, Norman barons built many castles. They were mostly of the motte-and-bailey kind. A curtain wall stood around the bailey. Towers were built at the corners of the wall and at intervals along the sides. Soldiers could use the towers as safe bases. The towers had a thicker belt of stone at the base. This was called a batter. It was there

◀ IRISH DEFENSES
The high towers of Ireland were built as refuges from invading Vikings. They were not intended to hold out against a long siege but were good look-outs and safe places to hide.

▶ BAMBURGH CASTLE
Bamburgh Castle Keep, in Northumberland, England, dates from 1200. The keep was the strongest part of a castle.

THE KEY TO THE CASTLE
The gate was the most vulnerable part of a castle because it was the point of entrance. When it was open, attackers could force their way in, and the castle could be captured very quickly. It was very important that the opening could be closed quickly. An iron gate called a portcullis could be dropped into place in seconds. The drawbridge only needed to be lifted a short way to prevent the enemy crossing the moat.

▶ DRAWBRIDGE
The drawbridge was made from very thick wood. It could be raised very quickly. It was operated by a system of weights which worked in the same way as a see-saw.

◀ PORTCULLIS
The portcullis was operated by a winch. The guards could release it quickly, and let it crash down under its own weight. Spikes on the bottom of the portcullis could trap attackers caught underneath it.

to strengthen the towers against battering rams and make it difficult to mine through the walls.

The gate was the weakest part of the castle. It was protected by a gatehouse and a portcullis. Some gatehouses had two portcullises. Attackers could be lured through the open gate only to find their way barred by an inner portcullis or gate hidden around a corner. Once the attackers were inside, the defenders would lower the outer portcullis and trap them. The passage between the gates became a stone tunnel. In the roof of the tunnel were slots known as "murder holes." Defenders could shoot arrows, drop rocks or pour boiling oil or water through the holes on to their trapped enemies.

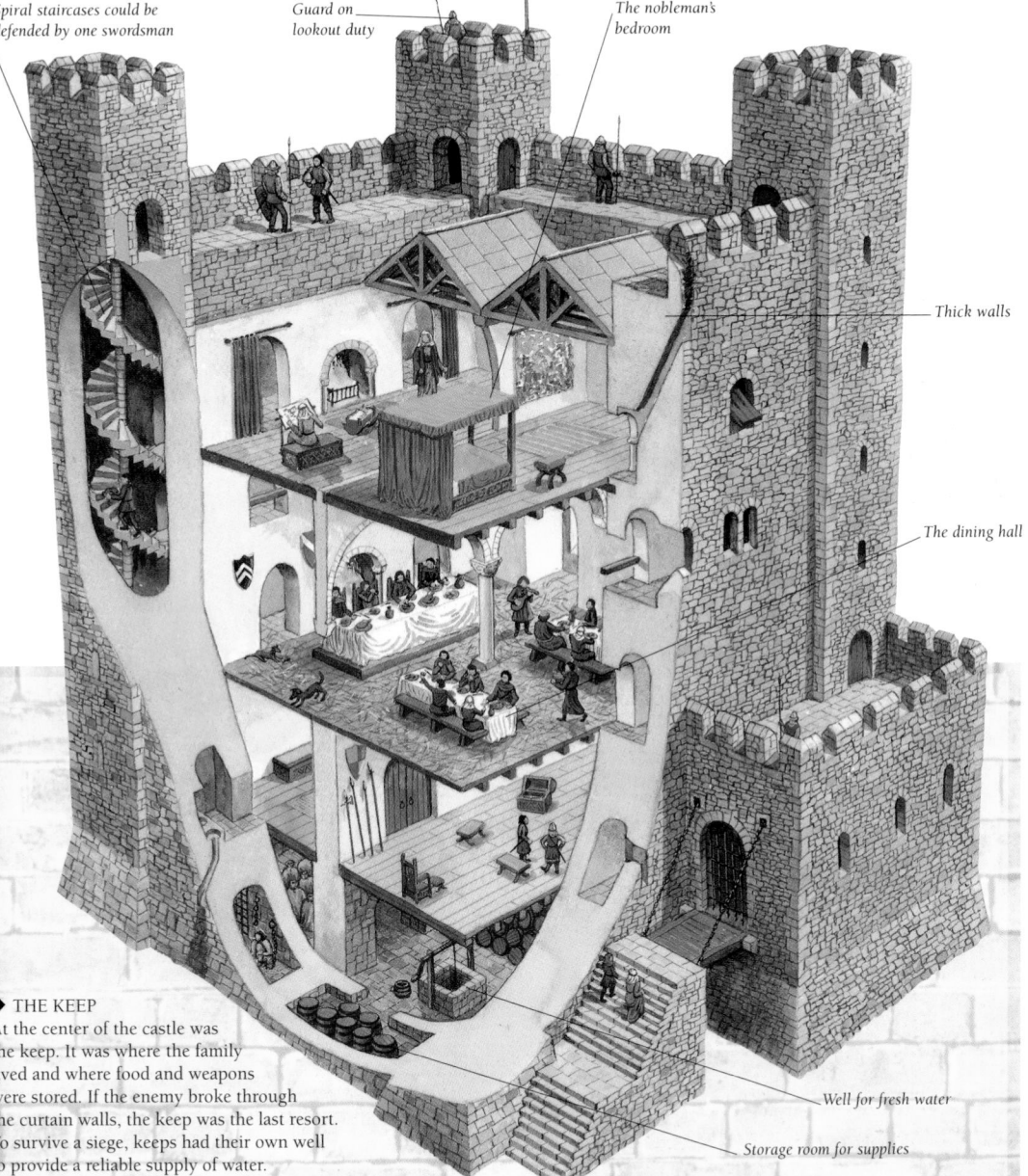

Spiral staircases could be defended by one swordsman

Guard on lookout duty

The nobleman's bedroom

Thick walls

The dining hall

▶ THE KEEP
At the center of the castle was the keep. It was where the family lived and where food and weapons were stored. If the enemy broke through the curtain walls, the keep was the last resort. To survive a siege, keeps had their own well to provide a reliable supply of water.

Well for fresh water

Storage room for supplies

Walls

Castle walls were built to a set pattern. Surrounding the castle was a curtain wall. This could be fifteen to twenty-five feet thick and wide enough for people to walk along. On top of the wall was the parapet. The parapet was a wall about one-and-a-half feet thick. In some castles they were built only at the top of the outer face of the wall. Others had them on both sides. They were about six feet high, so that they completely concealed and protected any soldier standing guard on the curtain wall.

Along the parapets were regular gaps which were low and wide enough for an archer to shoot at enemies. The gaps were called crenellations. The sections of raised wall between the gaps, which protected the archer, were called merlons.

At intervals in the wall and in towers of the castle, the builders cut narrow windows from which archers

▲ KEEPING THE NIGHT WATCH
Castles were defended day and night. Norman soldiers on the parapet check on the sentries manning the gatehouse and curtain wall defenses below.

could fire. These were called embrasures. When soldiers began to use cannon, the embrasures were made larger to fit the muzzles of the guns. Circular holes were cut at the base of arrow slits so that both the artillery men and the archers could fire from the same embrasure. This embrasure was known as a "cross-and-orb."

Larger embrasures were covered by hinged shutters when they were not being used. From the outside, an embrasure looked like a narrow slit. On the inside, it opened up so that an archer could lean to one side and shoot at targets to the left or right. A variation on this design was the balistraria, a cross-shaped slit for crossbows.

If an enemy force reached the base of a wall the defenders had to lean out to attack them. This would leave them open to attack by enemy archers. The castle builders invented machicolation, which was made to

SLITS AND EMBRASURES

The walls and crenellations of castles were pierced with holes called embrasures. These were made so that the soldiers could fire arrows or crossbow bolts at their enemy below. Later, castle walls were pierced with loopholes for cannon and muskets. The hole was shaped to fit the kind of weapon being fired through it. On the inside face of the wall the sides of the embrasure were angled so that an archer or musketeer could shoot at targets to one side.

▼ ARCHER'S SLIT
The earliest kind of slit was made to fit arrows. Arrow slits also let light and air in to the inside of the castle and through the curtain walls.

▲ CROSSBOW EMBRASURE
This design was used by crossbow archers. It allowed them to aim at targets to the left or right of them, or even to track a moving target before firing their bolts.

▼ LOOPHOLE
When cannons began to be used, arrow holes were changed to fit them. A round hole was cut at the base of a narrow slit.

◀ CARCASSONNE
This walled city in southern France looks much the same today as it did in medieval times. With such strong defenses, the only way an enemy could capture the city would be to starve the citizens.

▲ WINDSOR CASTLE
The towers on each side of the gatehouse at Windsor have machicolations at the top.

protect the defenders. This was a battlement wall built out on stone supports. It had embrasures that faced downward so that defenders could drop rocks and stones on their attackers.

Henry VIII made many changes in the design of fortresses. To fight off the threat of French invasion in the mid-16th century he built a number of forts along the south coast of England. Their walls were not high, but low and massive. This was to provide a wide platform for cannons and large guns to stand on. As the power and range of cannons got better, the walls of fortifications became wider and lower.

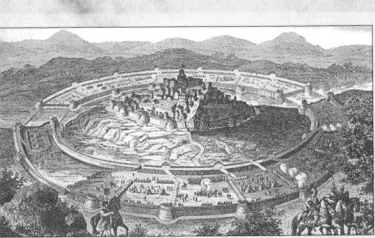

◀ WALLS WITHIN WALLS
The Roman general Scipio, also known as Africanus, built a wall with seven forts around the Spanish city of Numantia. He then besieged the city for eight months in 133 B.C. Its 4000 citizens finally gave in after Scipio had blocked off the river access.

▶ CITY WALLS
In ancient times cities were often under threat of attack and invasion. It was common to build fortified walls around the city for protection. This imposing wall surrounds the Morrocan city of Essaouira.

Key Dates

- 1451 B.C. Walls of Jericho stormed.
- 598 B.C. Nebuchadnezzar destroys the walls of Jerusalem.
- 493 B.C. Piraeus, the port of Athens, made secure with fortifications.
- 478 B.C. Athenian city walls restored.
- 457 B.C. Athenian long wall built.
- 393 B.C. Conon rebuilds long walls at Athens following their destruction by the Persians.
- A.D. 93–211 Walls of Perge (southern Turkey) built by Septimus Severus.
- 447 Ramparts of Constantinople rebuilt after earthquake.

Defending Borders

▲ THE GREAT WALL
Large enough to be seen from space, this famous earthwork in China took centuries to build.

▶ HADRIAN'S WALL
Named after the Roman Emperor Hadrian, the wall was originally a wooden palisade with a bank and ditch. It was later rebuilt as a stone-faced wall 16 feet high and 8 feet thick. Small emplacements, called mile castles, were placed at every mile along the wall.

MOST FORTIFICATIONS in ancient history have normally protected families and their retainers in castles, or citizens behind curtain walls with fortified gates. When the movement of large numbers of people threatens a civilization, bigger walls have to be built. The Great Wall of China and Hadrian's Wall in England are two very famous examples of land barriers made to defend whole territories.

The Great Wall of China was built over four distinct periods. The building of earthworks in 476–221 B.C. was followed by the Great Wall of Qin Shi Huangdi (221–206 B.C.). The Great Wall of Wu Di (140–86 B.C.) and other emperors was finally finished as the Great Wall of the Mings (A.D. 1368–1644). The Great Wall of China was originally built to delay Mongol attacks along the north frontier long enough for the main force of the Chinese army to get to the threatened area and defeat the enemy.

The Roman Emperor Hadrian toured northern Britain in A.D. 122 and ordered the construction of a physical barrier against the lawless tribes in Caledonia (modern Scotland). At first, the barrier was made from

Roman legionary

THE WORLD'S EDGE

The Romans and the Chinese had huge empires to guard. Just beyond their borders were people ready to invade. To mark and defend their borders, they built long walls or earthworks. A system of signaling allowed sentries to alert the garrisons if raiders tried to cross the wall. Then soldiers could quickly get to the site to drive them off.

◀ LEGIONARY FROM AFRICA
Roman soldiers were recruited from all parts of the enormous empire. They were often sent on duty far away from their home country. This was to make sure they did not desert.

▲ WALLS AROUND WALLS
The Romans used walls and ramparts as weapons in their siege tactics, closing off a city or fort from any outside assistance or supplies and starving it into surrender. This is the siege of Massilia laid by Julius Caesar in 49 B.C. Massilia is modern-day Marseilles.

◀ MILE CASTLES
Protected from the Picts (the painted people) from the north by Hadrian's Wall, small towns grew up around the mile castles along the wall. There were shops and markets, taverns and baths. Many of the Roman legionaries who manned the wall married and settled down in the towns.

timber and turf. In its final form, Hadrian's Wall was just a stone wall. It ran from Wallsend on the east coast to Bowness in the west, a distance of approximately 73 miles. The wall used natural features such as crags to give it extra height. It varied from 7 to 10 feet in width and was 15 feet high with a crenellated parapet 5 feet above that. There were mile castles along the wall at regular intervals of one Roman mile (4,856 feet) and two guard turrets between them. The mile castle was in a kind of gateway with a garrison of about 16 soldiers. The turrets may have been shelters for soldiers on guard or signal stations. Ten forts were built to house the garrison for the wall.

Hadrian's Wall was an effective military obstacle, and, like similar Roman barriers, it marked the limits of the Roman Empire. Beyond it were barbarians.

▶ JERUSALEM
The walls of the Holy City have been stormed and fought over ever since biblical times. Jerusalem is a city divided into the Jewish western area and the Arab territory in the east. Since the founding of the modern Jewish state of Israel in 1948, there have been frequent clashes.

◀ BUILDING THE GREAT WALL
During the Ming period, the wall was made from dressed ('finished') stone and brick. It was about 30 feet at its widest and varied in height from 25 to 40 feet. The parapet added an extra 5 feet. The top of the wall was wide enough for horses to gallop five abreast. Every 200 paces there were towers 12 feet high which straddled the wall. Crossbow archers could cover the gap between the towers north and south of the wall. Signal flags or beacons were used to pass messages between towers.

Key Dates

- 476–221 B.C. Various earth walls built in northern Chinese provinces.

- 221–206 B.C. Emperor Qin Shi Huangdi orders earth walls to be joined together to make the first Great Wall of China.

- A.D. 100 Romans build walls (called limes germanica) across Germany and Romania.

- 122 Emperor Hadrian orders wall to be built at northern edge of Roman Empire.

- 700s King Offa of Mercia, England, builds a dike to separate England from Wales.

Under Siege

▲ OUT OF RANGE
Building a castle on a hill site with a moat and a narrow, easily guarded entry road makes it very hard for an enemy to capture it.

A SIEGE IS WHAT happens when an enemy army surrounds a castle or a city planning to capture it. They can attack, or they can wait until the people inside get too hungry and surrender. A strong, well-stocked castle or fortified town could easily withstand a siege if their besiegers ran out of food. The defenders of a castle or even the wall around a town were higher up than the besiegers so they could see what the enemy was doing. They were also protected by a wooden palisade or a stone wall. From behind these walls, sniper archers could pick off the attackers as they came to the foot of the wall.

If the attackers reached the wall, they tried to make a hole in it so that they could get into the castle or city. Another way to get in was to climb the wall using ladders and grapnel hooks. This was dangerous, because the defenders waited until an attacker was half way up the ladder then pushed it away from the wall.

To attack the enemy camp the soldiers of the castle could use many of the weapons that the besiegers had been using. Each side lobbed rocks or cannon balls at

one another. If a battering ram was used, the defenders might try to set fire to it. Another way to disarm it was to use huge tongs hanging from a crane to grab the ram and pull it up inside the castle or curtain walls.

Castles often had secret passages leading to a hidden exit called a "sally port". This could be further down a river or along the coast and from here the defenders might make their escape if the siege became too severe. Sally ports were also very strong doors from which the defenders could launch quick raids on their attackers. The plan was to destroy the enemy's siege weapons, generally by setting them alight. The defenders would also capture prisoners and steal food stocks.

▶ HOT RECEPTION
As storming ladders are raised against a castle, defenders fight back by pouring boiling water or oil on the shed protecting a battering ram crew.

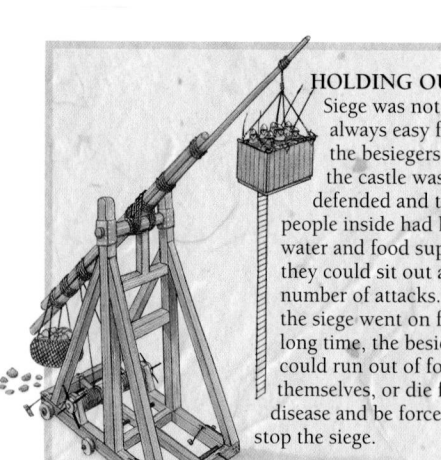

HOLDING OUT
Siege was not always easy for the besiegers. If the castle was well defended and the people inside had lots of water and food supplies, they could sit out any number of attacks. If the siege went on for a long time, the besiegers could run out of food themselves, or die from disease and be forced to stop the siege.

◀ SIEGE SEE-SAW
The tenelon was a crane or see-saw with a basket on one arm. Troops inside the basket could be hoisted over the walls.

▲ WHO'S WINNING?
Every kind of siege weapon is used against the defenders in this castle keep. They are fighting back but seem to be outnumbered and may be running o[ut] of food. One of the soldiers is lowering a basket and water pot for supplies.

◀ A CASTLE FALLS
Battering rams, scaling ladders and towers can all be seen in action in this medieval siege. It is the end of the siege. The walls have been finally breached after heavy bombardment and the besiegers are within the walls.

◀ ROMAN SIEGE
The Roman army were very successful at sieges. They invented many techniques and siege engines. In this scene, the besiegers are attacking on three points. A ram batters at the tower. Soldiers advance under cover of their shields locked into the testudo, or tortoise, formation. Some have reached the wall and are scaling it. A tenelon hoists men on to the far tower. The defenders crowd the battlements, but they only have rocks to throw at the enemy.

Key Dates

- 415–413 B.C. Siege of Syracuse. Athenians fail to take city.

- A.D. 70 Siege of Jerusalem, part of the Jewish Wars of the Roman Empire.

- 1189–91 Siege of Acre (Israel), part of the Third Crusade.

- 1487 Siege of Malaga.

- 1544 Siege of Boulogne.

- 1565 Siege of Malta, part of the wars of Islam. Turkish army try to capture Malta from Christian forces. They fail.

- 1688-89 Siege of Londonderry.

Siege Attack

THE ROMANS HAD A VERY SUCCESSFUL method of siege attack. First, they would take a good look at the target fort or city to see if a siege would be practical. They would then surround their objective with an outer belt of defenses so that it could not be relieved by friendly forces and set about systematically destroying it. Several specialty weapons were needed to do this. The most important was the siege tower.

Historic pictures of siege towers often show something that looks like a mobile multi-story building. The height varied. The three iron-clad towers used by the Romans in the Siege of Jerusalem in A.D. 70 were 30 feet high with catapults on top. The towers were fitted with drawbridges that were lowered to span the gap to the castle wall. The military engineers Gaston de Bearn and William de Ricou, employed by the Crusaders

in 1099 in another siege of Jerusalem, designed two towers of about the same height as the Roman towers.

The earliest descriptions we have of siege weapons come from around 400 to 200 B.C. Among them were those developed by the engineer Diades, who worked with Alexander the Great. Diades developed two unusual siege weapons, which do not seem to have been copied by future generations. The first one was a mural hook, also known as a crow. It was slung from a wooden gantry like a ram but it had a huge double

▶ **ANCIENT ATTACKERS**
Babylonian siege machines batter down the walls of an enemy fortress while archers fire on the walls.

Siege tower

Animal skin covering

Battering ram

▲ **SIEGE GRIFFIN**
A fantasy siege engine designed to be winched toward the enemy as it fires the cannon from its mouth. The ramp in the chest would be lowered for the assault.

SIEGE TOWERS
In order to reach the top of the walls and take on the defenders, soldiers had to be at the same height and within range. Mobile siege towers could be pushed forward until the soldiers inside them could fire at the enemy and eventually cross simple drawbridges onto the walls.

Mantlet

◀ **ALEXANDER**
Alexander the Great was a fine general. He laid many sieges. The best known was the Siege of Tyre, a fortified town. It lasted for seven months.

▲ **MOBILE SHIELD**
The mantlet was either a row of set hurdles, o in this example a mobile shield which could be wheeled clos to the enemy wall to give cover to archers.

lawed hook. This was used to pull down the battlements along the top of a city or fortress wall. The second was the telenon, a kind of crane. A large box or basket hung from it. Soldiers got into the basket and were swung onto the enemy's walls to attack.

Smaller items were also used. Scaling ladders were lightweight ladders, sometimes with hooks at the top. The besiegers used these to assault the walls. The soldiers would run forward, place the ladders in position and scramble up them.

Grapnels or grappling hooks were hooks attached to a length of rope. Soldiers would throw the grapnel so that it hooked over the parapet of the wall and then climb up the rope.

While the soldiers were climbing the walls, archers would keep shooting from behind their mantlets to keep the enemy occupied. Otherwise the defenders would just cut the ropes or push away the ladders.

Another way to get inside was by using a trick. In the Trojan War between the Greeks and the Trojans, the Greeks pretended to give up. They gave the city of Troy a large wooden horse as a parting gift. The Trojans took it inside the city, not realizing that there were Greek soldiers hiding inside the horse. Once inside the city walls, the Greeks jumped out and, after some fighting, they took the city and won the war.

▼ GOING IN
The drawbridge on an Assyrian siege tower crashes onto the enemy wall as the assault party storms in.

◀ ENGINEERS AT WAR
The Romans were masters of the planning and building work as well as the tactics of a siege. The siege of a large city was like a major engineering operation. Large numbers of timber structures had to be made very quickly and put into position. Sieges could go on for many years so any building had to be quite sturdy.

Key Dates

- 612 B.C. Nineveh (modern Iraq), capital of the Assyrian Empire, besieged and destroyed.

- A.D. 1346-47 Siege of Calais. Town officials prepare to die following surrender.

- 1429 Siege of Orleans relieved by Joan of Arc.

- 1453 Siege of Constantinople. Turks take the city ending the Holy Roman Empire.

- 1871 Siege of Paris. Citizens driven to eat zoo animals.

Bombardment

▲ GETTING YOUR OWN BACK
In this medieval picture, trebuchets are used to lob the severed heads of prisoners over the walls of a castle.

BEFORE SOLDIERS had cannons, bombardment weapons were built based on natural forces.

Classical and medieval siege weapons worked on one of three principles: spring tension, torsion or counterweight. Spring tension weapons were like giant crossbows. They used springy wood that bent easily, such as ash or yew.

Torsion means twisting. Torsion weapons were powered by twisted rope. The tighter it was wound up, the more power there was when it was released. This method could be used to fire stones or javelins. The Romans of the 3rd century A.D. nicknamed one of their torsion weapons onager, meaning "wild ass." This was because of the violent kick of the machine's arm when the rope was released. They used a rope made from human hair for this weapon because it was very elastic.

The ballista was a little like a crossbow. The tension was produced by bending two lengths of wood held in coiled cord or braided hair.

The counterweight weapon or trebuchet reached Europe from China around A.D. 500. It was like a giant see-saw with a heavy weight at one end and a sling at the other. A stone or other missile was placed in the sling which was tied down so the heavy weight was in the air. When it was released, the weighted end would drop and lob the stone.

Stones were not the only thing that the trebuchet threw. Burning materials were hurled over the walls to try to start fires. Corpses of humans and animals were also thrown. This was to spread infection and to bring down the spirits of the defenders.

Looking at these weapons today, they seem crude and simple. However, in medieval Europe, with its poor roads and simple carpentry tools, building a weapon such as a trebuchet or a catapult and bringing it into action was a very impressive feat.

▶ WILD ASS
The onager or "wild ass" was developed about the 3rd century A.D. It earned its name from the violent kick from the throwing arm when the ratchet was released.

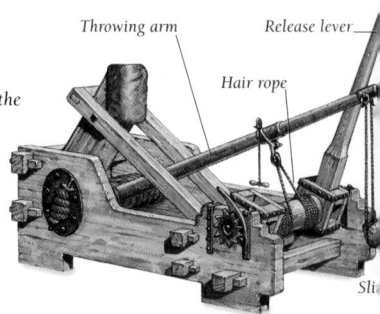

Throwing arm   Release lever
Hair rope
Sli

▲ ARCHIMEDES
A Sicilian scientist, Archimedes designed weapons for the defenders of Syracuse during the siege of 213–212 B.C. His engines were very effective against the Roman fleet.

GUIDED MISSILES
Before gunpowder, muscle power was used to throw missiles at the enemy. Soldiers had to be very strong to stretch or twist the ropes and springs or lift the heavy counterweights that gave catapults and trebuchets their power.

▶ GREEK FIRE
Siege machines could be adapted to throw "Greek fire," a mixture of chemicals, over the walls to burn the enemy.

◀ MASS ATTACK
This machine was designed to fire a barrage of arrows or javelins at one time. It was probably not very accurate.

◀ BALLISTA
The Romans developed the ballista, a weapon to launch missiles at the enemy. It worked rather like a crossbow and could be adapted to suit various kinds of ammunition. A light field ballista such as this could fire stones or javelins.

▼ CATAPULT
Protected by a mantlet, three soldiers tighten the tension on a catapult while a fourth prepares a stone for launching. The largest catapults could fire a 50 pound stone as far as 400 yards.

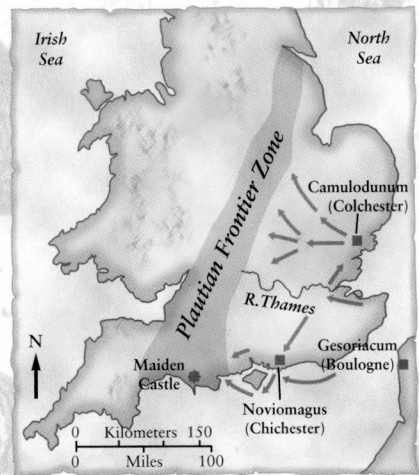

ROMAN INVASION
In A.D. 43, the Romans invaded Britain in the south. They got as far north as the Plautian Frontier, named after the Roman leader Plautus. Maiden Castle in Dorset was the site of a battle between the Britons and the Romans. At this battle, catapults and ballista were used by the Roman army. There had been a fort of some kind on this site since the Stone Age, but by the time the Romans came, it was well fortified by ramps, walls and dikes.

Irish Sea

North Sea

Plautian Frontier Zone

Camulodunum (Colchester)

R. Thames

Gesoriacum (Boulogne)

Maiden Castle

Noviomagus (Chichester)

N

0 Kilometers 150
0 Miles 100

Key Dates

- 400–200 B.C. Catapult introduced into Rome from Syria.

- 211 B.C. Mounted crossbow, possibly designed by Archimedes, in use to defend Syracuse.

- A.D. 100 Greeks build a catapult with an iron frame.

- 101–107 Ballista used by Romans in the Dacian wars (central Europe).

- 300 Onager in use with Romans. It was still used in medieval times.

- 1250s Trebuchet in extensive use.

- 1000–1400 Spring engines used in medieval Europe.

Ramps, Rams and Mining

So that they could bring their weapons in closer to the enemy, besieging troops built ramps outside the walls of the city or castle. Ramps or causeways were needed to cross ditches or moats filled with water. Ideally more than one ramp would be built so that the enemy would not know where the main assault was going to fall. The Romans pioneered the technique of building a ramp, known as an agger, from hurdles, packed earth and stone.

Once the besieging forces had filled in the moat and built a ramp up to the enemy's walls, the battering ram was wheeled into position. The battering ram was one of the oldest siege weapons. It was made from a heavy tree trunk hung on chains from a timber frame. The whole thing was covered by a wooden shelter called a penthouse. The roof and walls of the penthouse were often covered with animal hides that were kept wet as protection against fire.

The battering ram could have a metal knob, sometimes in the shape of a ram's head, that was mounted at the front end of the tree trunk. By swinging the ram and driving it against the wall, the soldiers operating it would, with time and effort, make a hole.

▲ ROMAN RAMP
The agger or ramp is protected by flanking towers. Soldiers work on the ramp under long protective sheds.

▶ UNDERMINING
Defenders could destroy a ramp by digging a tunnel under its wooden piles and setting fire to them to make the ramp collapse.

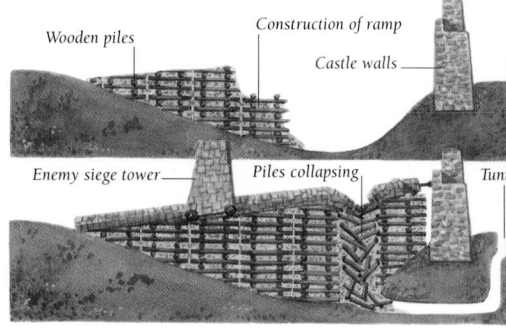

Wooden piles   Construction of ramp   Castle walls   Enemy siege tower   Piles collapsing   Tun

▲ GREEK BATTERING RAM
This wheeled tower is a two-in-one weapon. The ram batters the wall while the arm above it pulls down the castle battlements.

BATTERING TO VICTORY

The battering ram was the heavyweight siege weapon used to smash holes in the walls of a castle or town. There were many different designs. It was an accepted rule in Roman siege tactics that once the ram had been brought into action, the defenders within the fort or town could expect no mercy when the walls finally came down. So a ram was a frightening weapon in more ways than one.

◀ DEMONSTRATION
This picture shows how an 11th-century ram worked. In a real battle, the ramming crew would be protected from fire and missiles by a penthouse.

▶ RAM TOWER
Rams could be carried on the shoulders or mounted on wheels. This ram tower was pushed forward on wheels or rollers until it was within range of the castle wall. The gantry structure allowed the crew to develop a good, powerful swing with the ram.

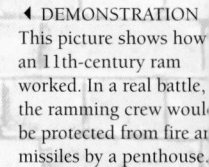

◀ HOOKING A RAM
A hook mounted on a crane grabbed the siege weapon, which could be lifted and dropped until it broke up.

Mining was another way to break through a city or castle wall. First, the attackers would build an easy-to-move shelter and put it against the wall. Protected under the shelter, the soldiers could begin to knock down the wall. They supported it with wooden beams so that it did not fall down too soon. When enough of the wall had been weakened in this way, a fire would be lit under the beams. When the beams had been weakened by the fire, the wall collapsed, and the besieging forces could then storm across the gap that had been created. The soldiers inside the castle could dig their own mine beneath the attackers' mine shaft. They could try to make the enemy's mine collapse, or fight underground.

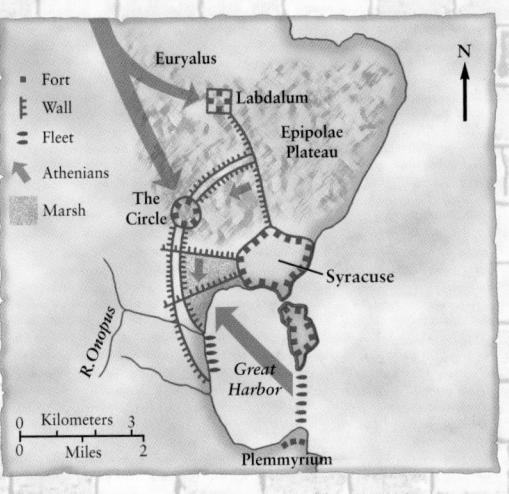

▶ SYRACUSE
The map shows the Siege of Syracuse in 415 B.C. by the Athenians. They built the square fort at Labdalum and a circular fort with surrounding siege walls. But Syracuse held out and inflicted Athens greatest defeat. The Athenians lost nearly 200 ships and 40-50,000 soldiers.

Map labels:
Euryalus
- Fort
F Wall
Fleet
Athenians
Marsh
Labdalum
Epipolae Plateau
The Circle
Syracuse
R. Onopus
Great Harbor
Plemmyrium
N
0 Kilometers 3
0 Miles 2

Key Dates

- 429–427 B.C. Plataea, in Greece, besieged using ramps and defeated by Spartans.

- 214–211 B.C. Siege of Syracuse (Sicily). Archimedes, born in Syracuse, designs some of the defense machinery.

- 52 B.C. Siege of Alesia in Gaul. Vercingetorix the Gaulish leader finally surrenders to Romans.

- A.D. 72 Siege of Masada, Jerusalem. Romans build ramps to get over the huge walls of the fortress. Many defenders choose to kill themselves rather than be captured.

Gunpowder Arrives

▲ POWDER RECIPE
The formula for gunpowder—one part sulphur, six parts saltpeter and two parts charcoal—was first written down by the Englishman Roger Bacon around 1242.

SOLID GUNPOWDER turns quickly into gas when burnt. If it is loose, gunpowder produces a flash, a cloud of white smoke and not much noise. If it is enclosed, the noise and the explosive force increases. This produces energy which can be used to push a solid object along a tube, or to blow up a building. The first use of gunpowder

in battle in Europe was by the British at the Battle of Crécy (1346). King Edward is said to have had three to five guns which were called roundelades or pots de fer because of their bottle or pot shape. Early weapons fired stones or arrows similar to crossbow bolts.

Cannon design did not change much over three hundred years. Gunpowder was poured into the open end or muzzle, and then packed down with a rammer. The packed gunpowder was secured in place with batting, which was rammed home. A cannon ball was then loaded. Loose gunpowder was poured down the touch hole, a small hole at the closed end of the cannon. It was lit using a slow match, a length of rope soaked in saltpeter, which would burn slowly. The explosion that followed pushed the cannon ball out of the gun muzzle. It could reach ranges of between

Penthouse

Cannon

Wooden frame

▶ WHEELED CANNON
Protected by a penthouse, this cannon sits on a simple frame that allows the crew to move it around the castle to fire stones at the enemy battlements. The cannon is held in place with guy lines and pegs which absorb the recoil when it fires and ensure it is correctly aligned.

EXPLOSIVES
Gunpowder was first used in Europe for weapons in the 14th century. It had been used in China since the 11th century to fuel battlefield rockets. It was more powerful than ropes, counterweights or springs, but gave off big clouds of smoke.

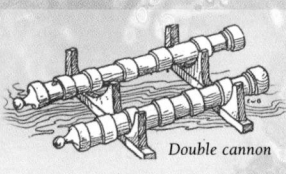

Double cannon

◀ DOUBLE SHOT
These cannons are on a stati[c] mount and would be fired ir[n] quick succession against a wall or gate—almost like a double-barreled weapon.

▶ HAND MORTAR
A 16th-century short-barreled weapon used for lobbing shot into enemy ranks.

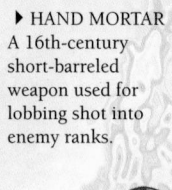

Hand mortar

▲ HAND CANNON
The hand cannon was first used in 1364 and was the first step towards hand guns as we know them today. The gunner had to support his heavy firearm with a forked pike to keep it steady.

▶ SNAKE GUN
This drawing by the artist Dürer shows a cannon called a serpentine as it was thought to look like a snake or serpent. Many early cast cannon were shaped to look like serpents.

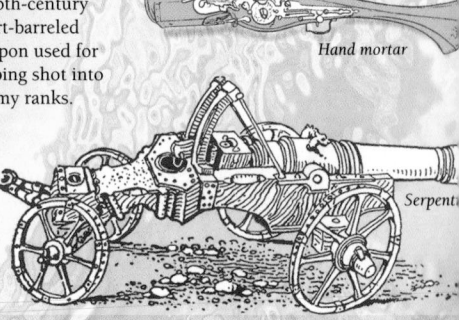

Serpent[ine]

20 yards and 765 yards depending on the size of the cannon and the ball. By the 1860s, ranges for a 12 pound cannon ball fired using a 2.5 pound charge had increased to 1,640 yards.

The ninth Siege of Constantinople by the Turks from April to May 1453 is the first example of the power of cannon. Constantinople was then the capital of the Eastern Roman Empire. It was ruled by Constantine XI. The Turkish leader was Sultan Muhammed II. A Hungarian engineer called Urban made a very long bronze cannon for the Turks.

◀ ENGLISH GUNS
One gunner raises the mantlet as the other prepares to light the touch hole to fire the stone ball.

▲ CANNON WITH COVER
Early cannon were built in a similar way to beer barrels. Lengthwise cast iron strips were bound with iron hoops and mounted in a static wooden carriage.

It measured 26 feet and was capable of throwing a 1,455 pound stone a mile. Loading and firing took some time, so the weapon could only fire seven times a day. After 12 days of heavy bombardment, the Turks had broken through the walls of the city. Constantinople fell on May 29, 1453.

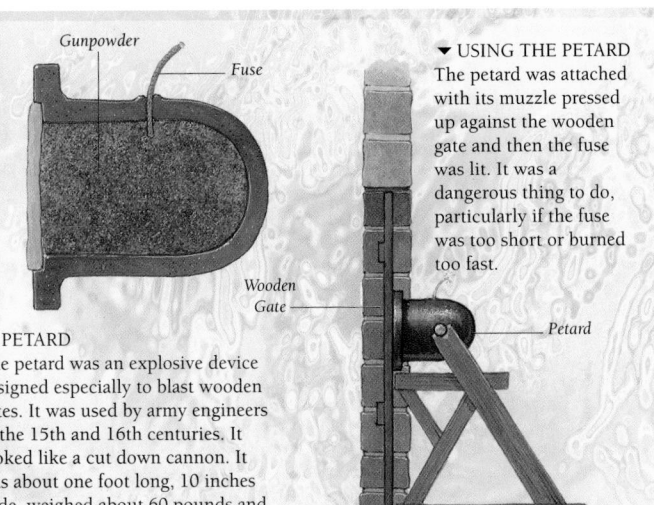

Gunpowder

Fuse

▼ USING THE PETARD
The petard was attached with its muzzle pressed up against the wooden gate and then the fuse was lit. It was a dangerous thing to do, particularly if the fuse was too short or burned too fast.

Wooden Gate

Petard

▲ PETARD
The petard was an explosive device designed especially to blast wooden gates. It was used by army engineers of the 15th and 16th centuries. It looked like a cut down cannon. It was about one foot long, 10 inches wide, weighed about 60 pounds and had a touch hole and open muzzle.

Key Dates

- 1242 Roger Bacon writes down the formula for gunpowder.

- 1324 Cannon believed to have been used at siege of Metz, in France.

- 1342 Reports of cannon at siege of Algeciras, Spain.

- 1346 Confirmed use of cannon at the battle of Crécy, France.

- 1450–1850 Most cannon were cast in bronze, iron or brass.

- 1500 Metal shot had replaced stone.

- 1571 At the battle of Lepanto, Greece heavily gunned galleys were used.

War at Sea

▲ OAR POWER
There were many kinds of warship design. This is a Greek galley with a single bank of oars.

THE MEDITERRANEAN Sea was central to the ancient world. Its name means "in the middle of the earth." Many countries depended on it for food and trade. Whoever controlled the sea therefore, had power over all the countries which surrounded it.

The Mediterranean has hardly any tides. Ships were not dependent on the tide coming in to launch and could not become stranded when the tide went out. The sea became part of the battlefield. Fighting methods and weapons were much the same as they were on land. The key to sea fighting was transportation. Fast boats with a reliable power source usually won the battle. The Greeks, Romans, Persians and Carthaginians all developed warships which could deliver troops quickly to the scene of the battle. As each would try to stop the other, they adapted land weapons for use at sea, such as grappling hooks, siege towers and catapults.

A good general used sea power to help his land battles. The tactics developed by the ancient sea

▼ OARS AT WORK
There were three layers of galley slaves in a trireme. To be effective they had to be able to row in time, so they probably used a drum to keep the time. Clearly the best position was on the top row.

SEA POWER
Most warships relied on banks of galley slaves to row them into action. Some ships had sails which could be used when the wind was favorable.

◀ XERXES
This Persian king came to power in 486 B.C. and launched a massive land and sea assault on Athens and her allies in 480 B.C. but he was defeated.

▶ THE BATTLE OF SALAMIS
This classic sea battle was fought in 480 B.C. between the Athenians led by Themistocles and the Persians under Xerxes.

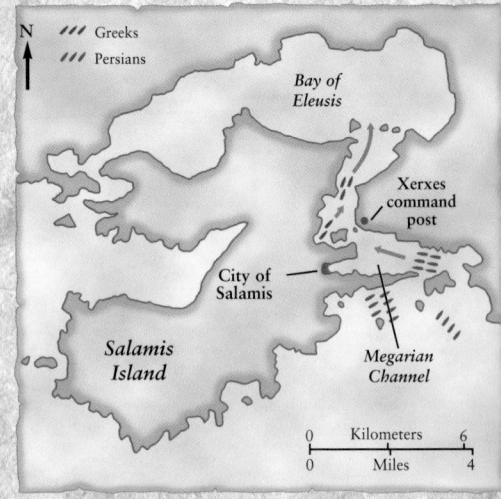

Greeks
Persians

N

Bay of Eleusis

Xerxes command post

City of Salamis

Salamis Island

Megarian Channel

| 0 | Kilometers | 6 |
| 0 | Miles | 4 |

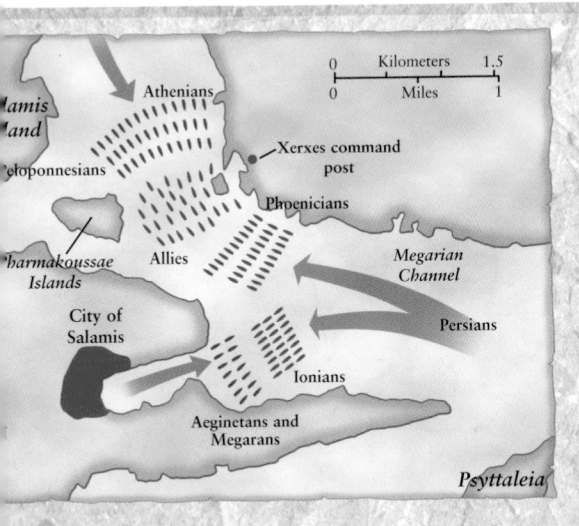

captains still work today. The Athenian plan for the Battle of Salamis was so successful that it is taught in miltary school. The sea battle at Lepanto in 1571 was fought between Austria and the Turks; it was the last time galleys were used in war. Austria captured 130 Turkish galleys and destroyed 80 more. The battle ended Turkish control of the Mediterranean.

Different kinds of ships and skills were needed to deal with larger seas, more extreme weather and tides. Countries with coastlines on the Atlantic or Pacific built boats that could land in shallow water if the tide was out. The Vikings who sailed the Atlantic owed their success to their long, flat-bottomed boats which could land almost anywhere.

Boats were used to deliver troops to a land battle or invasion. Vikings, Saxons, Danes and Normans invaded Great Britain by sea between 800 and 1066. During the Crusades in the Middle East, knights were brought from Europe by sea. Ships were also used to help in the sieges of coastal cities.

Kilometers 0 — 1.5
Miles 0 — 1

Athenians
amis
land
eloponnesians
Xerxes command post
Phoenicians
harmakoussae
Islands
Allies
Megarian
Channel
City of
Salamis
Persians
Ionians
Aeginetans and
Megarans
Psyttaleia

◀ TACTICS
The Persian fleet of 1000 ships had trapped the 370 Greek triremes in the Megarian Channel. The Greeks retreated northward, luring the Persians into the narrow waters near Salamis. Once there, the Persian fleet could not maneuver. The Greeks turned and went on the attack. They sank 300 Persian galleys and lost only 40 ships of their own.

Key Dates

- 486 B.C. Battle of Salamis. Greeks beat Persians.

- 31 B.C. Battle of Actium. Caesar Octavian defeats Mark Antony in Roman Civil War.

- A.D. 1340 Battle of Sluys between French and English as part of 100 Years War. Warships become battlefields.

- 1571 Battle of Lepanto. Austrians beat Turks.

- 1588 England defeats Spanish Armada.

Sail or Oar?

I N THE ANCIENT WORLD, trading ships used sails and windpower to move around the seas. Captains of warships could not rely on winds and tide alone. They used manpower as well. Greek, Roman, Turkish and Spanish ships used massed oarsmen. Others, such as the Anglo-Saxons, Norsemen and Normans, used a combination of sail and oars. The French and British preferred sail-powered vessels and improved their design through the centuries.

The Greeks were first with the oar-driven warship. They used vessels called triremes which had three rows of oars and 150 rowers. Athenian sailors developed a way of fighting using their rowing skills. They would approach an enemy ship at full speed, come alongside and at the last minute pull in their oars. This smashed

◀ ARMED GALLEY
A Roman sculpture shows the banks of oars with armed soldiers at the ready on deck.

▲ THE MARY ROSE
Henry VIII's flag ship was arm with cannons low down which could fire broadsides.

A HARD LIFE
Few people wanted to row a galley. Criminals in countries such as Italy or Spain in the 15th and 16th centuries were often condemned to the galleys as a punishment. Prisoners of war were also made to row in their enemy's galleys.

▶ OARS AT WORK
There were three layers of galley slaves in a trireme. To be effective they had to be able to row in time, so a drum was used to beat out the rhythm.

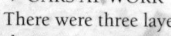

▲ GALLEY SLAVES
Chained to their benches in the dark, hot smelly hull of their boat, galley slaves could be worked until they died. Their bodies would be thrown over the side.

◀ MEDITERRANEAN GALLEY
Fast, light, unarmed boats were used to transport troops. If the boat was sunk in battle, the soldiers and the rowers were picked up by their own side and the boat was abandoned.

◆ FLOATING BATTLES
Spanish and English ships engage in battle in 1372 as part of the 100 Years War. The warships sailed very close together and the soldiers fought across the decks as if on land.

all the oars on the enemy ship, which were still sticking out.

The oarsmen in the galleys were normally slaves. Some were convicted criminals, but many were prisoners of war. By the time of the Battle of Lepanto (1571) the Turks had smaller galleys called galiots with 18 to 24 oars, and the Venetians had developed a large vessel called a galleas. Galleys were equipped with sails so that with favorable winds they could operate without using the oarsmen.

The Scandinavian raiders who roamed as far away as the Mediterranean and Black Sea used both wind and manpower. Under Bjarni Herjolfsson, a Viking longboat reached North America in A.D. 985. The Vikings could row their long, narrow boats when there was no wind or they were close inshore. Because the vessels were light and almost flat on the bottom they could land on gently shelving coasts or even mud flats.

By the 14th and 15th century, all warships in northern Europe relied on wind power. The sailors working in the tidal, stormy waters of the English Channel and North Sea needed to be very skillful.

Under Henry VIII ship design began to change. By the time of the Armada, British warships were sleek and low. They were about 115 feet long and 33 feet wide and were called galleons. Like the galley, they were ships built specially for war. New designs in sails and rigging made the vessels even more seaworthy. The galleon was able to make long distance voyages and so it became the vessel used by navigators and explorers.

▲ FAST AND FURIOUS
Vikings used their fast boats to make lightning raids. They were able to sail as far as America. The chance of plunder and easy targets made the risky journey worthwhile.

Viking warrior

Key Dates

- 241 B.C. Lilybaeum. After a long siege, Rome defeats Carthage, and Carthaginians lose 120 ships.

- A.D. 655 Battle of the Masts. Moaviah governor of Syria attempts to capture Constantinople from the sea.

- 841 Vikings reach Dublin.

- 1027 Normans land near Naples and establish stronghold.

- 1281 Mongol invasion of Japan defeated by "divine wind" or "kamikaze."

- 1588 Spanish Armada in running battles with the English fleet along the south coast of England.

Ramming and Grappling

BEFORE GUNPOWDER ALLOWED SHIPS to stand off at a distance and bombard one another, warships used light siege weapons, archers and slingers. The siege weapons could kill and injure people and damage sails and rigging. The archers and slingers acted as snipers, finding targets on the enemy ships.

Ramming could cause major damage. From the Greeks in 600 B.C. to the Spanish Armada of 1588, galleys powered by oars were fitted with a long ramming beak. The trick was to drive this into the hull of the enemy ship.

▲ SHIP RAM
This massive bronze-cased ram could easily pierce the hull of an enemy ship if it struck broadside.

▲ GREEK FIRE
Fire can be used as a weapon at sea. "Greek fire," an inflammable chemical, was used by Byzantine ships around the 4th century.

The Romans introduced a new weapon in 260 B.C. at the Battle of Mylae in Sicily. The corvus or "crow" was a hinged gangplank with a weighted hook. It could be swung out over an enemy ship and dropped so that it was stuck in the deck. Then a boarding party raced across the corvus on to the enemy ship. The Romans won at Mylae and took control of the Mediterranean.

Grappling irons, hooks with heavy chains, were later used in sea battles to assist boarding. Once the ships were alongside and the boarding parties in action, the fight became a land battle at sea, with hand-to-hand combat. Medieval ships showed this in their design with crenellated wooden "castles" in the bow and stern.

WAR AT SEA
Before gunpowder changed war, ships could ram the enemy, or slice off their oars. Other weapons were the corvus and twin-hulled siege vessels which could carry fighting towers.

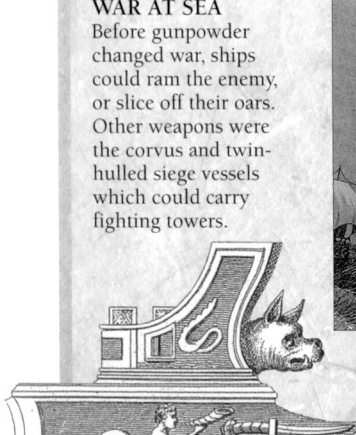

◀ DECORATIVE RAM
This finely worked prow with its ram shaped like a row of swords shows the quality of the work on classical warships.

▲ ROMAN SEA BATTLE
Some sea battles between the Romans and Carthaginians were on a huge scale, with ships locked together as boarding parties fought.

▲ FIRE SHIP
This ingenious little ship is designed to carry a tub of burning tar into the middle of an enemy fleet at anchor. It could damage rigging and sails and had the potential to sink ships much larger than itself. The English sent fire ships like this one against the Spanish Armada when it was at anchor.

► CROWS AND TOWERS
The Romans developed a grappling weapon called a corvus, the Latin word for crow. It looked something like a crow's big beak. It was a hinged gangplank with a hook which sank into the enemy ship's deck. Special twin-hulled siege vessels could carry fighting towers to the enemy.

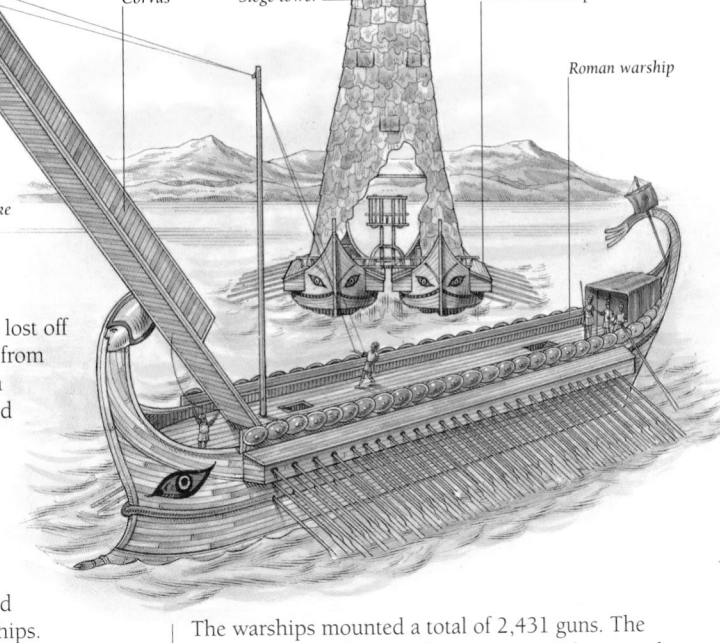

Corvus | Siege tower | Twin-hulled ship | Roman warship | Spike

This is why the front of a ship is known as the forecastle or fo'c'sle.

The English warship the Mary Rose, lost off Portsmouth in 1545, marks the change from ancient to modern warfare at sea. When she was recovered in 1982 from the mud into which she had settled, her weapons included both longbows and cannon. The ship was designed without castles but with gun ports on the lower decks. Heavy broadside cannons stood on these gun decks. When they opened fire, their shot would damage the hulls and masts of enemy ships.

In the running battle with the Spanish Armada in 1588, the English Royal Navy demonstrated that modern ship design, skilled sailors and good weather could shift the odds in favor of a smaller force. The Spanish had 20 great galleons, 44 armed merchant ships, 23 transports, 35 smaller vessels, four galleases (a double sized heavily armed galley) and four galleys.

The warships mounted a total of 2,431 guns. The English had 68 ships in Plymouth, a London squadron of 30 ships and an additional squadron of 23 in the eastern English Channel. Aside from seafaring skills and ship design, their strength lay in their 1,800 heavy cannons, mostly long-range cannons called culverins.

In running battles up the Channel the English finally prevented the Spanish from landing in England.

◄ ARMADA
Before dawn on July 28, 1588, the English sent fire ships into the Spanish fleet off Flanders as part of their running battle with the Armada. It forced the Spanish to cut their anchor cables. In the great sea battle that followed, only a storm prevented the English fleet from capturing or destroying 16 of the most damaged Spanish ships.

Key Dates

- 480 B.C. Battle of Salamis, Greece. Greeks defeat Persians.

- 262 B.C. Battle of Mylae, Sicily. Romans win and take control of the Mediterranean Sea.

- 241 B.C. Battle of Lilybaeum, Sicily. Romans defeat the Carthaginians.

- 31 B.C. Battle of Actium, Greece. Romans defeat Cleopatra and the Egyptians.

- A.D. 1571 Battle of Lepanto. Christian Allies defeat Turks.

- 1588 Defeat of the Spanish Armada by the English.

Sailing to War

CARRYING SOLDIERS AND THEIR WEAPONS, vehicles, horses and food by sea and landing them on an enemy shore is called an amphibious operation. Amphibious means able to work on land and in water. In ancient times, this was a simple operation. Coasts weren't always defended and boats were flat enough to land directly on sand or shingle shores.

As ships became bigger, they had to remain off shore and troops transferred to smaller boats before they could land. Horses could swim ashore on their own, but artillery and wagons posed an extra problem. In bad weather these operations could be dangerous and so sailors and soldiers looked for sheltered anchorages where they could land and unload in safety.

One of the earliest recorded amphibious operations were the Punic Wars of 264–241 B.C. between the Carthaginians, who lived in what is now Tunisia, and the Romans, in modern Italy. Both sides transported men and horses across the Mediterranean. The Carthaginian general Hannibal even took about 80 war elephants by ship from North Africa into Spain.

There were earlier operations. The most famous is described in Homer's Iliad, an epic poem that includes both myth and fact. To lay siege to Troy (a city located in what is now Turkey) the Greeks, under Agamemnon had to sail across the Aegean Sea. Archeological evidence of both Troy and the Trojan Wars dates the sea crossing to around 1200 B.C.

BATTLES BY LAND AND SEA
Islands could not be attacked without the use of ships. Sometimes the landings were the beginning of a long campaign. They could be part of the siege of a fortified port, or the means of escape for a battle fought on the coast. Vikings used their boats like a modern "getaway car," raiding a settlement and escaping quickly.

▲ HELEN OF TROY
The wife of the king of Sparta was so beautiful that her face was said to have "launched a thousand ships." She was kidnapped by Paris of Troy, which began the Trojan Wars.

▲ NATURAL LIFT
A Sumerian warrior uses an inflated animal skin as a float to help him to cross a fast-flowing river.

◀ TROOP CARRIERS
Boats like this one were used to ferry troops across the Mediterranean to fight battles on land.

At Marathon in 490 B.C. a Persian invasion fleet landed a force of 20,000 on the Greek coast near Athens. They were defeated by the Athenians, who numbered only 11,000, but despite heavy losses they were able to reach their ships and escape.

In Europe there was usually no need for soldiers to travel by sea. The waves of raids by the sea-going Saxons between A.D. 205 and 577 and the Viking raids between 800–1016 reached eastern England and northern France. They were not so much amphibious operations as military "smash and grab raids," The Anglo-Saxons and the Vikings eventually settled in the territories they had been raiding.

For island countries, such as Britain, that might be threatened by enemy landings, it was a good idea to build watchtowers and fortifications at the harbors and likely landing sites.

▲ THE NEW WORLD
In the 16th century, Spanish and Portuguese explorers sailed west and invaded large areas of South America.

▼ INVASION
In 1066, William of Normandy transported 9000 men with all their horses and equipment for his invasion of England.

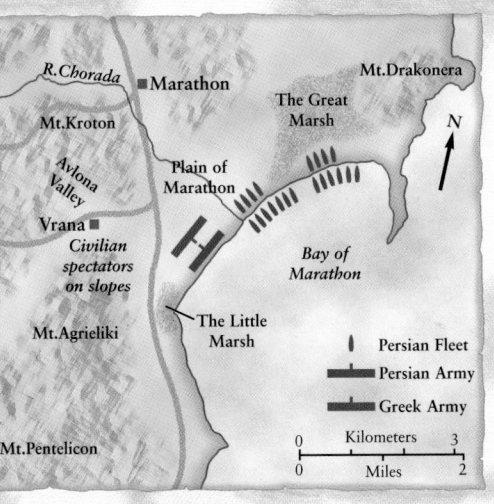

◀ THE BATTLE OF MARATHON
In 490 B.C. Persia invaded Greece. The Persian leader Darius worked his way down from modern day Turkey in the north, with a force of 150,000 men in ships. He landed an army 20,000 strong near Marathon. The Greeks met them on the coastal plain with about 11,000 soldiers and lost only 192 to the Persians' 6400.

Key Dates

- 490 B.C. Battle of Marathon. The Greeks defeat the Persians.

- 415 B.C. Athenians land in Sicily and besiege Syracuse.

- 54 B.C. First Roman invasion of Britain.

- A.D. 43 Second Roman invasion of Britain.

- 400s Raids on England by Jutes, Angles and Saxons.

- 700s–800s Vikings raid Europe.

- 1027 Normans land in southern Italy.

- 1066 Normans invade England.

Glossary

A

arquebus Muzzle-loading gunpowder weapon fired from the shoulder or supported on a tripod.

artillery In an army, large weapons which need transportation to move them around the battlefield and a crew of soldiers to use them.

B

bayonet A blade attached to the end of a musket, named after the French town of Bayonne.

broadside The side of a ship that can be seen above the waterline.

butt The end of a gun stock which is placed against the shoulder when the gun is being fired.

C

Crusades A series of campaigns led by Christian knights to regain the Holy Land (the area around Jerusalem) from the Muslims.

creese Malay dagger with a distinctive wavy blade.

cuirass Armor for the front and back of the upper body, originally made from leather.

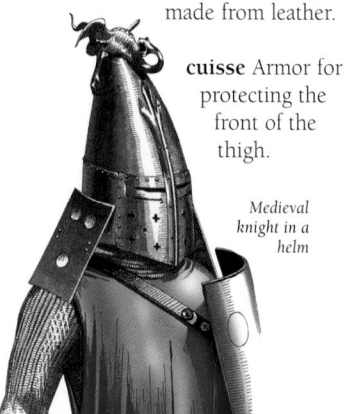

cuisse Armor for protecting the front of the thigh.

Medieval knight in a helm

E

emplacement The position of an artillery gun on the battlefield or outside a besieged castle.

English Civil War This conflict was between the supporters of the English king, Charles I (who were known as Royalists) and his opponents (called Roundheads) led by Oliver Cromwell. It took place between 1642 and 1648.

G

gisarme Medieval weapon based on a French weeding tool.

glaive Halberd with a blade that looks like a sword.

H

hand-and-a-half Heavy sword that could not be used easily with only one hand but was not quite as large as a two-handed sword.

hoplite An infantry soldier from ancient Greece who was heavily armed. Hoplon is the Greek word for tool or weapon.

I

infantry The soldiers who fight on foot with hand-held weapons. The infantry usually forms the largest part of any army.

J

jousting Sporting combat between two knights on horseback, fighting with blunt weapons. Jousts were often social gatherings.

K

knuckle duster or brass knuckles Slang word for a metal weapon worn on the hand over the knuckles. It gives extra power to a punch in a fist fight.

Norman soldier in chain mail

L

legionary Roman soldiers were called legionaries because they belonged to a legion. Legions were the main units of the Roman army. A legion contained between 3000 and 6000 infantry soldiers plus a cavalry unit.

linstock The stick or pole used to hold a length of slow burning cord that has been soaked in saltpeter, used to ignite the gunpowder.

Norman tower

M

medieval Term describing people, events and objects from the time known as the Middle Ages.

Middle Ages Period in history generally agreed to have lasted from around AD800 to 1400.

miguelet A Spanish flintlock firearm that has a mainspring and hammer on the outside. It was also known as a miquelet.

Mongol Word used to describe the people, events and objects of the Mongolian tribes who invaded Europe after the fall of the Roman Empire in the mid 500s.

musket A firearm which was loaded at the muzzle and had a smooth bore.

N

Norman Conquest The name given to the defeat of England by the Normans. William Duke of Normandy successfully invaded England in 1066, seized the throne and was crowned King William I on Christmas Day.

Fighting with double-edged swords

P

parry To deflect a sword thrust from an opponent.

pauldron Piece of armor made to cover the shoulder.

pistol Firearm designed to be used with one hand. It has a short stock, or handle, and barrel.

poleyn Piece of armor made to protect the knee.

Besieging a castle

pommel The weighted end of the handle of a broad sword, used to deliver a hammer blow in battle.

Punic Wars Three wars that were fought between Rome and Carthage over the territories of the Mediterranean region.

R

rampart Wide earth mound built to fortify a castle or town. It usually had a parapet on top.

S

saltpeter A mineral known as potassium nitrate. It is used to make gunpowder, explosives, matches and fertilizers.

Samurai A word first used to describe the imperial guard of ancient Japan. Later it was used to describe the warrior class in general. Warriors could only be Samurai by birth.

snaphaunce A firearm with a snap or spring lock.

Spanish Armada An armada is a fleet of battle ships. The Spanish Armada was a fleet sent by Philip of Spain that tried to invade England in 1588 but was not successful. The fight was over Spain's rich territories in southern America.

Spartan Word describing people, events and objects from Sparta, a city-state of ancient Greece.

squire A trainee knight aged about 14. He carried the shield and equipment of his instructor, attended to his horse, and defended him in battle. He was taught courtly as well as military skills.

stock The wooden grip or handle of a firearm.

Stone Age Period before the Bronze Age (around 5000 years ago) when stones and flints were used to make tools and weapons.

Swiss Guard Group of Swiss soldiers chosen to guard the Pope. The tradition was begun by Pope Julius II in the early 1500s. Today, a Papal Swiss Guard is still used to guard the Pope.

T

tournament Armed contest between medieval knights, fought for honor and ceremony.

trident Fork with three prongs.

trireme Warship used by ancient Greeks. Its name comes from the Greek words for "three" and "oar," because it was driven by men rowing three ranks of oars.

Index